CAPITALISM

Capitalism

THE STORY BEHIND
THE WORD

MICHAEL
SONENSCHER

PRINCETON UNIVERSITY PRESS

PRINCETON & OXFORD

Published by Princeton University Press
41 William Street, Princeton, New Jersey 08540
99 Banbury Road, Oxford OX2 6JX

press.princeton.edu

Library of Congress Cataloging-in-Publication Data

Names: Sonenscher, Michael, author.
Title: Capitalism : the story behind the word / Michael Sonenscher.
Description: Princeton, New Jersey : Princeton University Press, [2022] | Includes bibliographical references and index.
Identifiers: LCCN 2021059890 (print) | LCCN 2021059891 (ebook) | ISBN 9780691237206 (hardback) | ISBN 9780691238876 (ebook)
Subjects: LCSH: Capitalism. | Capitalism—Political aspects.
Classification: LCC HB501 .S77425 2022 (print) | LCC HB501 (ebook) | DDC 330.12/2—dc23/eng/20220224
LC record available at https://lccn.loc.gov/2021059890
LC ebook record available at https://lccn.loc.gov/2021059891

British Library Cataloging-in-Publication Data is available

Editorial: Ben Tate and Josh Drake
Production Editorial: Lauren Lepow
Jacket Design: Karl Spurzem
Production: Danielle Amatucci
Publicity: Alyssa Sanford and Kate Farquhar-Thomson

This book has been composed in Arno

Printed on acid-free paper. ∞

Printed in the United States of America

10 9 8 7 6 5 4 3 2 1

CONTENTS

v

PART II. SOLUTIONS 75

PREFACE

BEFORE THE EXISTENCE of both the concept and the reality of capitalism, there was once something called "commercial society." This book is about the similarities and differences between the two terms, starting with the one that is the more recognisable. Capitalism, wrote the author of a book that was published with much the same title as this one, first in 1917 and then in 1927, is a "political and polemical" term that has no place in the language of scholarship. But, as one of his reviewers pointed out caustically, the assumptions underlying the claim seemed to mean, therefore, that words like "religion," "liberty," or "patriotism" also had no place in the language of scholarship because they too could be taken to be political and polemical terms. Nor, the same reviewer continued, did the polemical character of the term, or the fact that the word itself could not be found in the first volume of Karl Marx's *Capital*, amount to anything like a real obstacle to finding out how to understand the difference between a capitalist and a noncapitalist society.[1] Capitalism might well be hard to define, but it was still quite easy to see.

Nothing much, it seems, has changed. Capitalism is a nineteenth-century word with a twenty-first-century charge. Although it is still quite hard to define, it remains quite easy to see. One reason for this mixture of the obvious and the opaque is the range of subjects encompassed by the word. Capitalism certainly calls for capital, but it is not quite so obvious that it also has to call for capitalists rather than, for example, organised businesses, managerial hierarchies, paid workers, multiple consumers, limited liability, incorporated stock, financial services, competitive markets, and bureaucratic states. Capitalism also seems to call for industrial organisation, technical specialisation, and the division of labour, but it is not quite so obvious that it also has to call for markets, prices, profits, and dividends. Capitalism, finally, seems to call for producers, products, and processes, but it is not quite so obvious that it also has to call for coercion, classes, and conflict.

Sometimes it seems to have called for them all, but it seems never to have done so all at once or settled into something fixed and determinate all at the same time and all in the same place. Capitalism clearly has something to do with making things, whether making cars or making money, but capitalism itself is not ready-made.

Capitalism, in short, is a compound term. In this respect it has something in common with the many different clusters of concepts, values, and ideologies that have, for example, been given the names of communism, nationalism, socialism, liberalism, conservatism, feminism, imperialism, or environmentalism. Capitalism is one of them. Like them, it is a word that ends in "-ism" and, as a nineteenth-century dictionary put it, this means that it has a systemic quality. Words ending in "ism," the dictionary noted, referring here to the word *atheism*, were "systemative," meaning that they indicated "a system, a doctrine, a way of acting, thinking or doing things."[2] Although, as another authority pointed out in the course of discussing the word *realism*, the ending made the words "excessively vacuous," it was still likely that they would "be used by the public as markers or milestones" to make it easier to label or classify people or doctrines because this, remarkably, was what the ending could do.[3] Behind the generic quality of the ending, however, there was still an endless variety of conceptual content and a ramifying array of overlapping genealogies of semantic origin. In this respect too, capitalism is one of them.

One of the aims of this book is to describe how the many heterogeneous components of the concept of capitalism came to be crystallised as a single word. This, in the first instance, calls for identifying where the different ingredients of the compound came from and, second, for explaining how, when, where, and why they came to be connected to and articulated with one another. Part of this story has already been told, initially by Richard Passow, the author of the book mentioned in the first paragraph of this preface, and in somewhat more detail in a now-forgotten article published in 1940 by a Swiss historian named Edmond Silberner in the prestigious French historical journal *Annales* edited by Marc Bloch and Lucien Febvre. In this article, Silberner showed that capitalism began as a French word, coined in the ninth, 1850, edition of a famous pamphlet by the French socialist Louis Blanc

entitled *Organisation du Travail* (or "The Organisation of Labour" as the English-language translation was entitled).[4] Although Silberner did not
explain why Blanc began to use the term or what
he intended it to mean, he did, however, single
out the fact that, in coining the word, Louis Blanc
made a point of juxtaposing capitalism to capital.
"Cry out," Blanc wrote, "long live *capital*! Long
may we applaud it and long may we go on to attack *capitalism*, its mortal enemy, with even more
intensity. Long live the goose that lays the golden
egg and long may we protect it from anyone seek-
ing to eviscerate it."[5]

It is not usual now to think of capital and capitalism as mortal enemies. One of the further aims of
this book is to try to show what this meant and
begin to explain why the conceptual opposition on
which it was based has come to look so strange.
The initial reason for both can, however, be set out
briefly here. This is the fact that Silberner's discov-
ery was not entirely accurate because, long before
Louis Blanc made use of the term in 1850, both the
word and the concept of capitalism were initially
associated with the related subjects of power politics, war finance, and public debt. The word "capitalist" actually began as an eighteenth-century

French word (*capitaliste*) that was usually applied to someone who lent money to one or other of the many branches of the French royal government to fund the costs of war. The original English-language equivalent of a *capitaliste* was, therefore, an annuitant or a stockholder rather than a capitalist. The English word came later. As will be shown in later chapters, the opposition between capital and capitalism on which Louis Blanc drew was bound up with this earlier usage. Gradually, however, the earlier usage also came to be bound up with a number of other clusters of concepts, values, and ideologies that, cumulatively and sequentially, came to form the moral and political context in which both the word and the concept of capitalism first arose. Some were connected to the subjects of property, inequality, and what came to be called the social question. Others were connected to the subjects of industry, the division of labour, and global trade. Still others, however, continued to be connected to the subjects of money, credit, and public debt. From the vantage point of eighteenth-century usage, however, capitalism did not have to wait for the publication of *The Communist Manifesto* to acquire the apocalyptic aura that it still can have. The aura was there right from the start.

One reason why this aura has lasted is that alongside the concept of capitalism there was another concept with a rather different set of connotations. This was the concept of commercial society. It had rather less to do with the subjects of war and debt that, as will be shown, formed the original context in which the concept of capitalism first appeared because the concept of commercial society was associated instead with the subject of the division of labour. Over the course of the nineteenth century, however, the two concepts began to merge. Discussions of capitalism in the context of the subjects of war and debt sometimes gave rise to predictions of either the end and dissolution of established political societies or the establishment of a universal empire under the aegis of a powerful and determined royal or republican government. Discussions of capitalism in the context of the subject of the division of labour also gave rise to predictions of either the end and dissolution of established political societies or the establishment of a domestic political empire, this time under the aegis of a new incarnation of a Roman Caesar as the combined effects of economic inequality and social isolation took their toll. The modern concept of revolution encompassed them both. The fusion gave an extra charge to the title of Marx's most famous publication, *The Communist Manifesto*, because a manifesto was, originally, the name reserved for a declaration of war. Quite a number of steps are required to explain how the subject of the division of labour came to be associated with the subjects of war and debt and, by extension, class war. One of the initial aims of this book is to describe how these steps occurred because several of them have now been forgotten. In the twenty-first century, the concepts of capitalism, commercial society, and the division of labour are usually associated with the economic and political thought of Adam Smith. In the early nineteenth century, however, the concepts of commercial society and the division of labour were associated as readily with the thought of a now much less well-known French royalist writer named Louis de Bonald. *The Communist Manifesto* brought the two sets of concepts together. The analytical starting point of this book is, therefore, a question about whether the concepts of capitalism and commercial society were, in fact, the same. It is followed by a further question about how to think about politics if, in fact, they were not.

The two questions derive from a third, more fundamental, question. This question arises from the conceptual overlap between capital, war, and debt on the one side and capital, commercial society, and the division of labour on the other. It is a question about whether what has come to be called capitalism was initially understood to be something that could offset or neutralise, rather than magnify or exacerbate, the effects of the division of labour. This is because the apocalyptic aura now usually associated with capitalism was initially associated with the concept of commercial society. In this respect, Louis Blanc was the inadvertent intellectual heir of Louis de Bonald. Capitalism, Blanc asserted, was the mortal enemy of capital. To Bonald, writing two generations earlier, the mortal enemy was commercial society. Others, however, like the Austro-German-Danish political economist Lorenz von Stein, took a different approach. If capitalists and capital were once associated with warfare, they could also be associated with welfare. From this perspective, the real mortal enemy, in Louis Blanc's terminology, was neither capital nor capitalism, but the division of labour. Capitalism in its original meaning was the solution, not the problem because capitalism in its original guise had more to do with public credit and state expenditure than with private property and competitive industry.

In this conceptual setting, capitalism was something more than a compound term because it was also substantially more morally and politically ambiguous than it now seems. Simply setting the names Blanc, Bonald, and Stein alongside one another helps to indicate that there were more than two sides to the initial array of arguments over capitalism. This was more than a matter of the difference between warfare and welfare because it was also a matter of a broader set of differences over economic, financial, monetary, legal, and political arrangements and institutions. Over time, many of these earlier differences and ambiguities have been lost because many of the questions that gave rise to both the word and the concept of capitalism have disappeared from historical view. By 1918, when Richard Passow published the initial version of his *Kapitalismus, eine begrifflich-terminologische Studie* (the book mentioned in the first paragraph of this preface), the initial sequence of questions about the similarities and differences involved in thinking about commercial society, the division of labour, and capitalism had already been largely forgotten. Here too, it seems, nothing much has changed. The subjects of commercial society and the division of labour belong largely to economic history or to the history of ideas and the history of social, economic, and political thought. The subject of capitalism belongs largely to Marxism or to global history and the new historiography of capitalism.[6] This book is about what, analytically, came before these several, apparently self-contained, types of historical understanding and, more substantively, about what was involved in thinking about commercial society, the division of labour, and capitalism during the period when these three, initially separate, subjects began to be defined and discussed before, over time, they turned into one. Its aim is to indicate what thinking about politics is likely to involve once historical investigation has begun to prise these overlapping subjects apart. A summary of the argument of the whole book can be found in the final two paragraphs of the first chapter.

ACKNOWLEDGEMENTS

I WOULD NOT have been able to piece together the information that I have used in this book without the opportunities provided several years ago by a senior research fellowship from the Leverhulme Trust and, subsequently, by the Institut des études avancées in Lyon and the libraries that I was able to use both there and in Cambridge. I am very grateful for the help I have been given both in those libraries and by the librarians of King's College during the present pandemic. I would not have been able to make use of any of the information that I have acquired without what I have learned from conversations with many members of King's College and, particularly, Richard Bourke, John Dunn, Lorna Finlayson, Basim Musallam, Rory O'Brien, Christopher Prendergast, Sharath Srinivasan, and Gareth Stedman Jones. One other title of this book might have been "The Economic Limits to Politics," the title of a book edited by John Dunn with a fine chapter in it by my late colleague Istvan Hont. I do not know what he would have thought of this book, but I do know that I owe some of its arguments to our conversations over the years. In a more immediate and substantive sense, however, I have a real debt to Maxine Berg, Edward Castleton, Graham Clure, Ludovic Frobert, Pat Hudson, Béla Kapossy, Isaac Nakhimovsky, Sophus Reinert, John Robertson, Keith Tribe, Richard Whatmore, and, above all, Charlotte Johann, for taking the time and trouble to answer my questions, read all or parts of earlier versions of the final text, tell me where I have gone wrong, and show me how I could have done things better. Elizabeth Allen helped me to improve the preface just at the right time and, generally, has encouraged me to keep going. Ben Tate and his colleagues at Princeton have been helpful and considerate advisers, collaborators, and producers. I am particularly grateful to Lauren Lepow also at Princeton for her editorial and technical advice in the final stages of the production process. The limitations and shortcomings of this book are, of course, my own.

PART I

Problems

I

Capitalism and Commercial Society

BEFORE THE EMERGENCE of the concept of capitalism, there was an earlier concept called "commercial society."[1] The link between the two concepts, it has usually been said, can be found in the thought of Adam Smith because this, initially, was where the two concepts of capital and commercial society can both be found. There were, it has also been said, two main reasons for the existence of this link. The first was that Smith's concept of commercial society was the fourth of a sequence of stages made up of the various ways by which human societies have acquired their means of subsistence, a sequence that started

with hunting and gathering, proceeded with rais-
ing livestock like sheep and cattle, continued
with agriculture and settled communities, and
culminated with commerce and industry. A commercial society was, therefore, what came after
hunting, pastoral, and agricultural societies. The
second reason was that the concept of commercial society fed readily into the concept of capital
that played so substantial a part in Smith's best-
known work, *An Inquiry into the Nature and
Causes of the Wealth of Nations* of 1776. Commerce generated capital, just as capital generated
commerce, which meant, from this perspective,
that a commercial society was simply a society
predicated on capital.[2] It was, therefore, a capitalist society or, in short, capitalism.

In fact, however, a commercial society was not
actually a society predicated on capital but, as
Smith himself wrote, a society predicated on the
division of labour, a phrase that Smith seems to
have coined, even though the concept itself was
well-established by the time that he wrote the
Wealth of Nations. "When the division of labour
has been once thoroughly established," Smith
wrote at the beginning of the fourth chapter of his
book, "it is but a very small part of a man's wants

which the produce of his own labour can supply. He supplies the far greater part of them by exchanging that surplus part of the produce of his own labour which is over and above his own consumption, for such parts of the produce of other men's as he has occasion for. Every man thus lives by exchanging, or becomes in some measure a merchant, and the society itself grows to be what is properly called a commercial society."[3] The scale and scope of the division of labour, Smith observed, was limited by the extent of the market.

"As it is the power of exchanging that gives occasion to the division of labour," he wrote in the first sentence of the preceding chapter, "so the extent of this division must always be limited by the extent of that power, or, in other words, by the extent of the market."[4] The division of labour and the market were therefore two sides of the same coin. They, not capital, were the initial, or primary, components of a commercial society. Capital came next.

Smith did not make use of the term "commercial society" at all frequently, but, on the two occasions on which he did actually use the term, he used it to describe the attributes of a society based on the division of labour. "The education of the

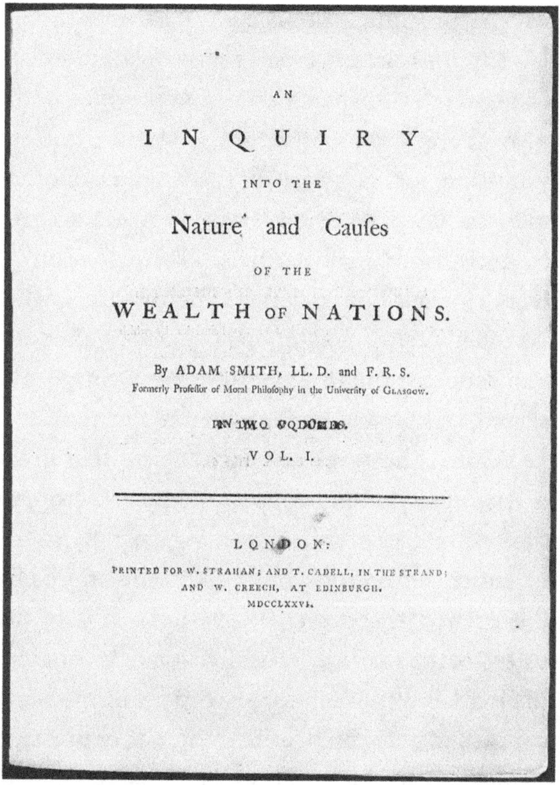

AN

I N Q U I R Y

INTO THE

Nature and Causes

OF THE

WEALTH OF NATIONS.

By ADAM SMITH, LL. D. and F. R. S.
Formerly Profeffor of Moral Philofophy in the Univerfity of GLASGOW.

IN TWO VOLUMES.

VOL. I.

LONDON:

PRINTED FOR W. STRAHAN; AND T. CADELL, IN THE STRAND;
AND W. CREECH, AT EDINBURGH.
MDCCLXXVI.

FIGURE 1. Adam Smith, *An Inquiry into the Nature and Causes of the Wealth of Nations* (1776)

common people," he wrote on the only other occasion on which he used the term, "requires perhaps, in a civilized and commercial society, the attention of the public more than that of people of some rank and fortune."[5] This was because people of "some rank and fortune" usually received an education before they began to work, but "the common people" began to work at an early age and the work that they did was often too time-consuming, routine, and repetitive to be compatible with the growth of knowledge, understanding, and curiosity that education could supply. Something like the publicly funded Scottish parish school system, Smith wrote, was consequently required to provide early education in "a civilised and commercial society."

If, as it is sometimes assumed, a "commercial society" is simply a synonym for "capitalism," where does this leave the division of labour? One of the main aims of this essay is to show that there is a great deal more to think about—and find out about—by beginning with the idea that capitalism and the division of labour are two quite distinct subjects. It is, of course, very easy to conflate the two because the division of labour and capital are, certainly, closely related. But they are not quite so closely related as either the concept of capital or the phrase "the primitive accumulation of capital" have usually been taken to suggest. In this account of their origins, capital and the accumulation of capital began with war, conquest, and slavery, making capitalism the product of slavery or, alternatively, the product of feudalism or, in other renditions, the disintegration and differentiation of household production into capital ownership by men and proletarian reproduction by women.[6] But, if conquest gave rise to capital, it is less clear why capital should give rise to the division of labour rather than, simply, to more conquest. Predatory societies do not need the division of labour to accumulate capital because, for them, capital is simply there for the taking. In this sense, as two of Smith's near contemporaries, Montesquieu and Rousseau, both argued, the accumulation, distribution, and redistribution of capital was in fact the other face of despotism. A despot could accumulate capital by imposing slavery and, subsequently, could go on to enjoy that capital unless or until it was seized by the next despot. The dynamics of capitalism and slavery were, therefore, rather different from the dynamics of the division of labour. The former did not need to involve markets; the latter did.

Smith himself was well aware of the need to provide a separate explanation of the origins of the division of labour. As he described it, the market-oriented disposition to truck, barter, and trade (he gave the three words almost the same meaning) that was the key to the division of labour grew out of the human capacity for rhetoric and persuasion. Anyone who could talk someone into doing this, rather than that, was, inadvertently, launching the division of labour. "If we should enquire into the principle in the human mind on which this disposition of trucking is founded," Smith said in one of his earlier lectures on jurisprudence, "it is clearly the natural inclination every one has to persuade."[7] As several of his contemporaries began to show, this initial, largely individual, capacity to see an opportunity and turn it to broader advantage could, subsequently, become more general and durable. One of the most plausible conjectures was set out by one of Smith's most attentive early French readers, the marquis de Condorcet, at the beginning of his posthumously published *Outline of a Sketch of the Progress of the Human Mind.*

There, the original causal mechanism underlying the formation of the division of labour was connected, first, to the size of human kin groups and, second, to variations in the ages at which people died rather than to something as generic as an individual capacity to use persuasive language. In these conditions, the early death of a patriarch, the absence of other adult claimants to the goods left by the defunct, and the presence or absence of large numbers of helpless children could produce windfalls for some and hardship for others.[8] Demography could, therefore, give rise to deficits or surpluses of different sizes and composition, and they in turn could become the basis of either the division of labour or the accumulation of capital or, sometimes, both.

There were many late eighteenth-century variations on this type of conjectural account of the origins of the division of labour and its relationship to the accumulation of capital. Here, it is enough to emphasise that the two subjects were historically and analytically distinct. On Smith's terms, a commercial society was, substantively, a society predicated upon the existence of the division of labour and not, at least in the first instance, on the prior existence of capital. This made the division of labour, not capital, the real historical novelty and the real basis of a commercial society. Although capital was also central to the existence of a commercial society, its more fundamental component was, as both Smith and Condorcet indicated, its relationship to the division of labour. Unlike capital itself, the division of labour presupposed markets, and markets, in turn, entail prices. Markets and prices are relentless and remorseless because, unlike capital, they are not the types of thing that can really be owned. As the old Latin distinction between *imperium* and *dominium* that used to be applied to the concept of property helps to show, markets and prices could certainly be subject to commands and rules (*imperium*), but they were still not the types of thing that could be physically occupied or possessed in the way that a house or a field or even a body can be owned (*dominium*). This raises several intriguing questions about the concept of capitalism. Where did the concept come from? When and where it did it begin? What did it add to the concepts of capital or a capitalist, which both existed long before the appearance of the concept of capitalism? How was capitalism different from Smith's concept of a commercial society? If, as seems likely, it really was, was it because capitalism was predicated on something different from the division of labour, such as, self-evidently, the private ownership of capital? If capitalism was a property theory, was the concept of a commercial society a theory of the division of labour, and, if so, what difference to thinking about both or either does this make? Was capital once seen as something that could neutralise markets? And, if capital was not a source of stability, how could markets be managed? In the light of Smith's identification of a commercial society with the division of labour, and the later identification of a commercial society with capitalism, what would the history of capitalism look like if the two subjects of capital and the division of labour were distinguished more fully and treated in ways that made it possible not only to explain how they interacted but also why they have come to be so readily conflated?

The aim of this essay is to try to provide some answers to these questions. Before capitalism, it aims to show, there was once a clearer conceptual distinction between capital and the division of labour than has become usual now, and this distinction was originally the basis of a number of different ways of thinking about how capital could be used to manage, neutralise, circumvent, or simply live with the power of markets. The answers to the earlier list of questions are, therefore, certainly designed to throw more light on the concept of capitalism. But they are also designed to throw more light on several other equally widely used concepts in the history of political thought. These include the concepts of justice, rights, property, and personality, as well as the many different levels of particularity and generality separating the material from the immaterial, the real from the ideal, and the concrete from the abstract that are the hall marks of complex political societies. All of them are relevant to the subjects of capitalism and the division of labour because of the mixture of the personal and the impersonal that they both contain. Both are made up of people and property, but both also rely on markets and prices. At first sight it seems to be the first that is the more deep-seated because people and property involve subjects like rights, responsibilities, and accountability in ways that are less directly or immediately connected to markets and prices. In fact, however, the opposite is more likely to be the case.

Property can be associated with almost anything. We own our bodies, just as we own our phones, even if the two types of ownership entail different types of rights, responsibilities, or entitlements. This is because the entitlements or responsibilities of ownership can be applied both to real people and to more impersonal agencies like a state, a fund, a partnership, a company, a corporation, a guild, a church, a parish, a team, a university, a foundation, or a trust. Over time, perhaps, any of these different types of ownership could change radically and could, conceivably, simply disappear into a cloud of electronic entitlement. The division of labour is just as likely to change, but it is not nearly so clear what its disappearance would entail. This suggests that capitalism could be more fluid than it looks, while the division of labour might be more deep-seated than it seems. It also suggests that Adam Smith, with his concept of a commercial society, recognised something more fundamental about its attributes and qualities than the later concept of capitalism has been able to grasp. It has not been difficult to identify or to advocate alternatives to capitalism. Over time, these have been called socialism, communism, associationism, cooperativism, collectivism, social democracy, state capitalism, or, less enticingly, national socialism. There is no reason to think that there will not be many more if only because the capital that is part of capitalism could belong to many other possible types of owner, such as a goal or a purpose as much as an organisation or a person. Our names are our own and we do, in a sense, own our culture even if it is not particularly clear what the content of that culture might be or what, in causal terms, helps to make it our own. The ubiquity of property is, in short, the other side of the indeterminacy of ownership.

It seems to have been much harder, however, to identify an alternative to the division of labour. At best, the concept seems to have generated one or two synonyms such as, for example, the concept of industrialism or, perhaps, even Hegel's concept of civil society. This absence of alternatives suggests that it has actually been much harder to avoid the finality of the division of labour than to imagine an alternative to capitalism. As Smith emphasised, the market, not capital, was the first sign of the division of labour. Markets involve commodities and prices; capital involves ownership and property. It is easy to identify many forms of property, but not quite so easy to identify many forms of a price. It could, in fact, be claimed quite plausibly that thinking about the division of labour came to an end in Europe and the United States at the beginning of the twentieth century with the thought of Emile Durkheim, Gabriel Tarde, Georg Simmel, Georg Jellinek, and Max Weber. Since then, there have been sociology, economics, political science, and anthropology on the one side and a proliferating array of critical studies in philosophy, psychology, literature, aesthetics, and other subjects on the other. Over time, the subject of capitalism has swallowed up the division of labour. There have, as a result, been many examinations of politics in capitalist society, but far fewer examinations of politics in commercial society.[9] Since, however, the concept of commercial society both differed from, and came before, the concept of capitalism, it might be the case that starting with the question of politics in commercial society is the way to bring back a number of topics that have been written out of the subject of capitalism because of the recurrent propensity to conflate commercial society and the division of labour with capitalism and property. This has made it harder not only to deal with capitalism and the division of labour as subjects in their own right but also to think about how they interacted, or were made to interact, in a number of different historical settings. Taking a step back may be the way to take a step forward and throw a new and different light on the once separate presence of capitalism and the division of labour in the history of modern political thought.

This essay is divided into two parts. The first part is an examination of the subjects of capital, capitalism, and the division of labour as they were described and discussed in the first half of the nineteenth century. The aim of this part is to show how the subject of commercial society turned into the problem of capitalism. The second part of the essay is a more thematic examination of a number of different ways of thinking about politics in commercial society before the subjects of the division of labour and commercial society were swallowed up by the concept of capitalism. Here the initial starting point is supplied by Marx and then, as a more historically grounded starting point for the subsequent discussion of the relationship between the concepts of capitalism and commercial society, by the thought of Adam

Smith. This time the focus is not so much on Smith himself as on a number of early nineteenth-century examinations of the relationship between justice and expediency in Smith's economic and political thought. This examination of Smith's intellectual legacy, and, in particular, Smith's concept of political society as it was described by several of his early readers, is followed by two complementary chapters: one dealing with the subjects of the state, government, and administration as they were discussed by the German political philosopher Georg Wilhelm Friedrich Hegel, and the other dealing with the subject of comparative advantage in international trade as it was discussed by the British political economist David Ricardo. Both pairs of subjects involved thinking about public debt, a subject that was taken up and discussed after the revolutions of 1848 by another German, but Austrian, political thinker, Lorenz von Stein, as the basis of his concept of social democracy.

The aim of the whole sequence is to describe how and why these different subjects came to be conceptually connected and, once the connections began to be made, to show why the outcome added up to a surprisingly comprehensive picture of modern political societies. The starting point of the sequence was Smith's distinction between justice and expediency. That distinction became the basis of Hegel's distinction between the state and civil society. That second distinction, however, called for something to bridge the gap between the state and civil society. This, as Hegel showed, was why the subject of the administration mattered because it was the administration that was the missing link between civil society and the state. The next step came from the subject of administration because an administration had to pay the costs of both administrators and administration. This, as Hegel's follower Stein showed, was why public debt and public finance had to be seen as key components of an administrative system. Public finance and public debt gave rise to a further step because they also set economic limits on domestic politics, and, as Ricardo and his followers began to show, these limits generated an incentive to find ways to base foreign trade on the concept of comparative advantage. There is, in short, a real historical and analytical gain to be made by starting an examination of capitalism with the subjects of commercial society and the division of labour. Before capitalism became a problem, the problem of commercial society began with the subject of the division of labour.[10] Getting the sequence right may be a way to turn the old questions raised by the problem of commercial society into a new set of answers to the problem of capitalism.

II

Capitalism and the History of Political Thought

NOT MANY WIDELY USED political concepts have come down from the nineteenth century. Republicanism, we now know, was either Greek or Roman or Hebrew in origin. Liberty, we have learnt, existed before liberalism. The concept of representative government can be found in Hobbes, Locke, Montesquieu, and Rousseau, while the idea of the separation of powers is usually attributed to the American Founders. Modern democracy, it is said, started with Spinoza. The distinction between sovereignty and government began, apparently, with Bodin, Hobbes, or Rousseau, while theories of human rights, perpetual peace, and international relations began with Kant, Sieyès, Wollstonecraft, Paine, and Bentham.[1] Only two concepts now seem to belong unequivocally to the nineteenth century. One is the distinction, first made by Benjamin Constant but amplified substantially by Isaiah Berlin, between positive and negative liberty and, in an overlapping sense, between ancient and modern liberty.[2] The other is the concept of capitalism. The concept is now usually associated with the thought of Karl Marx and, in Marx's wake, with Max Weber.

In fact, however, Marx made no use of the term "capitalism" because in his eponymous book he relied instead on the noun *das Kapital* to indicate the object of his analytical and political investigations. Weber's famous essay "The Protestant Ethic and the Spirit of Capitalism" clearly made more frequent use of the term, but he approached the subject of capitalism from a distinctly Nietzschean and value-oriented starting point, not only because of his own scepticism towards Marxism but also because of his still-underexplored intellectual engagement with the thought of his contemporaries and near contemporaries, notably

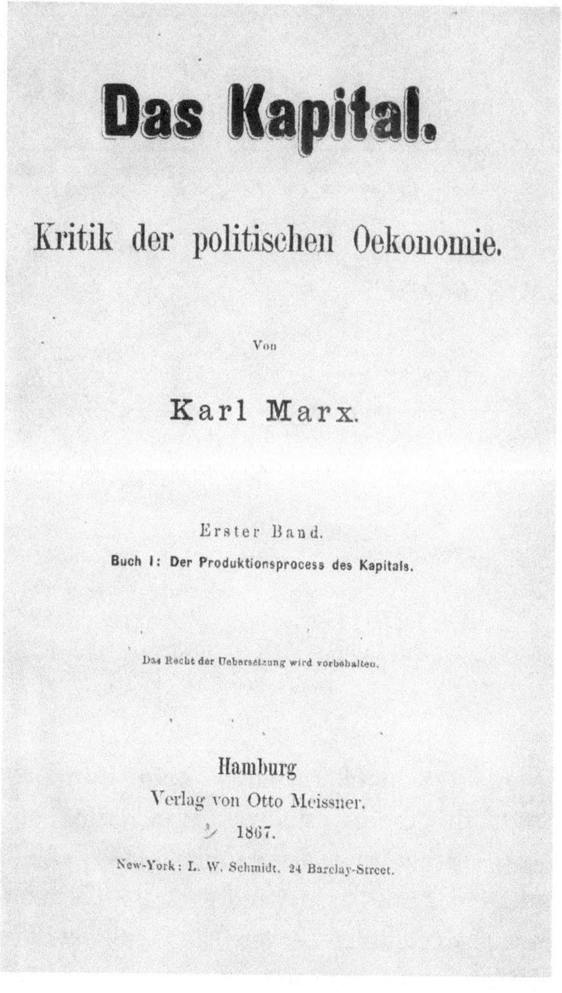

Das Kapital.

Kritik der politischen Oekonomie.

Von

Karl Marx.

Erster Band.

Buch I: Der Produktionsprocess des Kapitals.

Das Recht der Uebersetzung wird vorbehalten.

Hamburg

Verlag von Otto Meissner.

1867.

New-York: L. W. Schmidt. 24 Barclay-Street.

FIGURE 2. Karl Marx, *Das Kapital* (1867)

FIGURE 3. Max Weber, "Die protestantische Ethik und der
‚Geist' der Kapitalismus," *Archiv für Sozialwissenschaft und
Sozialpolitik* (1905). Left: the title page of the issue of the
periodical in which Weber's essay appeared. Right: the table of
contents of that issue.

Sombart, Schmoller, Dilthey, Simmel, and Jellinek.[3] They too were students of capitalism (Sombart, with his *Der moderne Kapitalismus* of 1902, is
still sometimes associated with the German-
language origins of the word), but they were also
the intellectual heirs of several earlier investigations of its nature and attributes.

Capitalism, in fact, began as *capitalisme*, or as a French-language term that began to become current at about the same time in the nineteenth century as the overlapping distinctions between positive and negative liberty and ancient and modern liberty also became current. The coincidence was more than chronological. It formed the substance of a discussion of the relationship between capitalism and liberty that began in France around the time of the July revolution of 1830 and seems to have continued ever since. In this discussion, one argument was repeated recurrently. This was that the type of liberty that is compatible with capitalism was not actually compatible with liberty itself. In this argument, the type of liberty that—with many still frequently unrecognised reservations—Constant called negative liberty, or the liberty of the moderns, was bound to be trumped by capitalism. The reason for this was that capitalism gave rise to forms and levels of inequality—between rich and poor, propertied and propertyless, rulers and ruled, colonisers and colonised—that clashed radically with justice, freedom, welfare, decency, or any of the many other ways of describing human entitlement that have been defended or defined. If negative liberty was bounded liberty, with limits imposed upon state power and government interference, capitalism itself was unbounded. Ultimately, according to this argument, the unbounded would undermine the bounded, generating crisis, oppression, or worse and leaving revolution as the one real alternative to the negative version of liberty that was all that was housed by existing arrangements. On the terms built into this argument, states, laws, governments, constitutions, institutions, organisations, and associations were all, ultimately, causally dependent upon the relentless vicissitudes of capitalism.

The coincidence between the new formulation of liberty as either positive and ancient, or negative and modern, and the emergence of capitalism as both a word and a concept was, therefore, substantive as well as chronological. Although the coincidence has usually been recognised in most historical writing more implicitly than explicitly, its significance has usually been described in two different but considerably better-known ways. One approach has been to claim that the coincidence highlights a real problem about capitalism that has been either intermittently forgotten or recurrently glossed over by capitalism's apologists. A second approach, however, has been to argue that it is not so much the essential properties of capitalism that have been forgotten or glossed over as its mutability, adaptability, and plasticity. The name might be the same but the thing itself has changed. In this rendition, capitalism, like almost all words ending in -ism, was not so much an entity in its own right as the name given to a nexus of economic, moral, and political problems whose content has changed radically and continuously over time. Their content changed, it is also usually claimed, largely under the impact of the various local or partial solutions produced by the magnitude, variety, or complexity of the different types of problem that capitalism has housed. Some problems were connected to wealth and power or the relationship between private power and public accountability. Others were bound up with markets and prices and their bearing on human capabilities and choices. Others were built into mechanised forms of industry and the interrelationship of work, wages, and different types of ownership. Some were related to the subject of political economy or the relationship between individual resources and the wealth of the state. Others were linked to the ownership or absence of ownership of property, whether individual, collective, or indeterminate. Yet others were associated with the relationship between morality and self-interest, while others were bound up with differences of race, class, gender, dependency, and empire. The list is long but could be much longer, because there is no reason to think that the proliferation of ever-transforming problems will end.

Capitalism, in this second rendition, was—and still is—heterogeneous, not uniform. Some problems, like bankruptcy and liability for bankruptcy, which were once taken to be intrinsic to capitalism, have been solved and, consequently, integrated into what, retrospectively, now seems to be part of its systemic properties. Some solutions on the other hand, such as those centred on the nature of property or money, have, inversely, given rise to new and unforeseen problems that cannot be found in earlier iterations of capitalism's problem-driven history. In this sense, capitalism could simply be said to be a word used intermittently to refer to a range of discrete and episodically connected issues bound up as much with politics and power as with class, industry, markets, or profits. From a third point of view, however, capitalism, despite its plasticity, has, somewhat surprisingly, remained the same word notwithstanding the many different issues and problems that it seems to have encompassed. From this perspective, what is unusual about capitalism is not so much that it has changed, but that the name itself still remains the same. Mercantilism and adventurism have come and gone, as too have industrialism, individualism, entrepreneurialism, or even commercialism, but capitalism has kept its charge. There is, therefore, a real question lying somewhere between capitalism's apparent heterogeneity and capitalism's putative uniformity. It is a question about whether, irrespective of any positive or negative evaluation, the subject of capitalism comes down to the same old story, or whether, perhaps, there is a better story to be told.

The better story calls initially for a switch of perspective. Instead of starting with capitalism and the question of its apparent heterogeneity or putative uniformity, the better, and more authentically historical, story calls for beginning with a question about the origins and nature of both these different characterisations of capitalism and the radically different types of *telos* that they appeared to entail. In the old versions of the story, capitalism was either one big problem heading towards a catastrophic outcome, or a compound of many heterogeneous problems with no determinate outcome. In the third version, it is not so much the subject of capitalism but the subject of catastrophe that came first. From this perspective, the real question is not so much whether capitalism was headed for catastrophe because, as it was put in a later phrase, of its internal contradictions, but rather whether the concept of capitalism, for all its apparent indeterminacy, was originally a more focused attempt to capture and describe a now-forgotten, but once better-known, cluster of conjectures about the nature of the modern world and the potential for catastrophe that it housed. Right from the start, in other words, something about capitalism was bound up with a more nebulous, but still quite specific, set of claims about history, teleology, and the several possible verdicts of history that the future promised to hold.

III

Capitalism, War, and Debt

THE FRENCH WORD *capitalisme* first began to be used in the third decade of the nineteenth century. At that time, its use was redolent of the eighteenth century and the more obviously personal noun, *capitaliste*, that began to appear, mainly after the War of the Austrian Succession of 1740–48, in French discussions of war and debt to refer to someone who supplied one or other of the branches of the French royal government with the capital they needed to fund the costs of war.[1] In this earlier usage, a capitalist was a person, while in later usage capitalism was a system. Initially, in the early nineteenth century, the overlap between the two terms was considerable. Among the commentators of this period was a once well-known journalist named Emile Morice, who had made his name by publicising the Parisian underworld characters of Vautrin and Vidocq now usually associated with the novels of Balzac, but who in this context was also the author of an essay on Holland and Belgium published in 1834 soon after Belgium established its independence from Holland. The relationship between the two countries, Morice wrote, was something like a duel, but not a real, weapons-based duel, because diplomacy would not allow it. It was instead "a commercial, economic, and fiscal duel" in which, unless something unforeseen occurred, victory would go to the "biggest bags of money" rather than, as Prussia's most famous eighteenth-century monarch, Frederick II, had once said, to "the biggest battalions." It was true, Morice continued, "that Holland can no longer count, as it could in the days of Jan de Witt, on a 10,000 strong fleet and 150,000 sailors, but it still disposes of a power of which Great Britain once had the monopoly. That power is capitalism and this is how this power was conquered":

In the age of its greatest prosperity, Holland not only took hold of the monopoly of the seas and of trade, but amidst all its wealth, it also contracted habits of order and parsimony that were to endow it one day with immense resources. Trade enriched all the classes of the nation; they all accumulated capital and, soon, having been the intermediary between Europe and distant lands, the Dutch became Europe's banker. No power failed to have recourse to its bourse and the dealers (*négociants*) of Amsterdam became the money suppliers and money managers (*argentiers*) of every sovereign.[2]

This transformation of traders into financiers, Morice explained, began to happen in the eighteenth century when the combination of growing reserves of capital and rising levels of taxation encouraged Dutch capitalists to look for more profitable investments abroad. By 1815 and the end of the Napoleonic Wars, the process had grown so much in scale and scope that the immense expenditure generated by more than two decades of global conflict gave rise to a worldwide credit squeeze that pushed up interest rates and revived the value of large quantities of discredited paper left over from earlier state issuance. Holland, with its huge capital reserves, was one of the beneficiaries of the resulting redistribution of financial resources, and, Morice wrote, although Belgium had established its nominal independence, it was easy to see that it would not be able to escape its real dependence on Dutch financial power.[3]

Belgium's limited prospects, Morice explained, were an effect of both the makeup of its own economy and the structure and composition of the other economies with which it could be expected to trade. Belgian textiles, for example, were certainly of as good a quality as those produced in Britain, but they were not as cheap. This meant that Belgian producers would not be able to export to the growing market in the United States unless the Americans were to give them a preferential tariff, which, however, would come at the price of making British textiles unavailable in the United States. This was very unlikely. France on the other hand could offer only competition, not outlets, because French textiles were used to offset domestic trade imbalances between the wine-producing French South and the wine-consuming French North and, in these circumstances, imported Belgian textiles could not be allowed to disrupt this function. A scenario involving French imports of Belgian textiles in return for French exports of French wine was, therefore, as unlikely

as a Belgian export surge to America. Further
north, the creation of the Prussian *Zollverein* was
likely to be more a threat than an opportunity to
the Belgian economy because it would block exports of Belgian coal but would also enhance the
viability and productivity of the many centres of
textile production situated within the German
confederation. Prussian living standards and
labour costs were, in particular, much lower than
those in Belgium, which meant that competitive
exports from Belgium to Prussia would be viable
only under the conditions of a highly implausible
fall in Belgian living standards and wage costs.

Matters were complicated further by the legal,
financial, and political ramifications of Belgium's
secession from Holland. In this context, what has
come to be called Brexit was preceded by Belgxit.
As Morice pointed out, Belgium's new sovereign
status raised a question not only about how much
of the earlier single Belgian-Dutch state's holdings
in external sovereign debt the new Belgian state
was entitled to own, but also about whether Holland might be expected to get compensation—
and if so, how much—for the loss of part of its
capital-generated income stream. As with the subject of trade, Belgium's own room for manoeuvre

was limited. It was not rich enough to afford the claims upon its tax revenue, and the broader industrial and agricultural sectors on which that revenue was based, to be able to compensate Holland without adversely affecting its own economy. Nor was there any prospect of help from the outside because, Morice claimed, neither Britain nor France would be willing to take over part or all of the Belgian debt. In addition, but from a different standpoint, neither Holland nor the German confederation would be willing to allow Belgium to have access to the benefits of a single market. Dutch canals and German rivers would now be only as accessible to Belgian merchants and shippers as they were to any other inhabitant of a foreign power. Uncertainty over the status of the Belgian public debt and the end of the single Belgian-Dutch common market would usher in a new age of tariffs and tolls, just at a time when the constitution of the new Belgian government was poised indecisively between a republic and a monarchy.[4] To Morice, the point of the analysis was self-evident. The Dutch government simply had to wait. Belgian independence would slowly give way to Belgian dependence. There was no need, as some feared, for the Dutch government to think about war to bring Belgium back under its control.

The concept of capitalism that Morice used in the early 1830s was clearly quite similar to many later versions of the concept. It drew attention to commercial competition and to the inequality and dependency that it brought in its wake. But it was also different from later usage in at least two significant respects. The first was the centrality of public debt and the part played by capitalists and the state in giving capitalism both its name and its nature. In contrast to later Marxist versions of the concept of capitalism, it was not so much the state that was the organised form of capitalist development as it was capital that was the organised form of the state's development, powered initially, and notably, by its military and naval development. In this early version of the causal relationship between capitalism and the state, the state came first, because it was the state's debt that formed the core of capitalism. Although there were several well-established eighteenth-century synonyms for the concept of capital, such as a stock, a fund, an undertaking, or an enterprise, indicating, contrary to an old claim found in histories of economic thought written by economists, that

the concept of capital did not have to wait for
Adam Smith or Turgot to be discovered, a capitalist, especially in eighteenth-century French
usage, was simply someone who invested in royal
and public debt. This has a bearing on the second
aspect of the concept of capitalism that Morice
used. In his version of the concept, the emphasis
fell firmly on international, rather than national,
trade and industry as something simultaneously
limiting the room for manoeuvre of any single
state but magnifying relationships of subordina-
tion and dependency between states. Economics,
in short, imposed limits on politics. The two
points are worth stressing because together they
indicate something significant in the odd mixture
of continuity and discontinuity underlying both
the name and the concept of capitalism. Although
it was called capitalism, it had, as Morice indicated, more than a little to do with the state. But,
despite this, it was still called capitalism and not,
for example, statism, even if the much later concept of state capitalism has allowed the capitalist
noun and the state-oriented adjective to coexist.
The semantic relationship between capitalism
and public debt also has a more substantive and
durable significance. This is because it makes it

possible to see more of a connection between capitalism and the related concepts of negative and positive liberty and the liberty of the ancients and the moderns than the truncated modern concept of capitalism has been able to supply.

IV

Capitalism, Royalism, and the Social Question

THE MOST VIVID ILLUSTRATION of the initial connection between concepts of capitalism and concepts of liberty can be found in another early presentation of the concept of capitalism, this time published in 1836 in a multivolume collection of memoirs and documents entitled *Mémoires tirés des papiers d'un homme d'état* compiled and edited by two French royalist journalists named Alphonse de Beauchamp and Armand François, comte d'Allonville. Here too the initial context was formed by the relationship between trade and politics. "The question of trade envisaged from a political point of view" was, according to a memorandum quoted by the editors of the compilation, "a particularly important question that has yet to be resolved."

> Born of the natural products whose venal value and ease of placement it facilitates, does it not, when it grows to be more extensive and moves towards its final term, produce two social vices that are as ruinous as they are corrupting? On the one hand, there is the superabundance of producers over consumers, which gives rise to inferior production. On the other, there is the substitution of a sterile traffic in gold and money in place of the vivifying flow of the products of agriculture and industry.[1]

Not much more, the memorandum continued, needed to be said about the imbalance between production and consumption because a just equilibrium could be expected to be established after the wave of inevitable misfortunes had passed. "But," its author exclaimed rhetorically,

> what is there to say about this new power of capitalism which, born of the trade that it ruins, has succeeded in all its immorality to the more moral power of fructifying the land that

it now oppresses by diverting capital from it? What is there to say about that power that sacrifices the future to the present and the present to that contemporary leprosy, individuality? What is there to say about that egoistical, cosmopolitan power which takes hold of everything, but produces nothing and is intimately connected only to itself? What is there to say about this sovereign of sovereigns who can neither make war without it, nor make peace with it, which enriches itself from both their prosperity and their ruin, from the goods belonging to the people that it shares and the evil done to them that it augments?[2]

At this point, Allonville, who by then was the editor of the series, added a long footnote to the text, noting that "this power" had only just come into being at the time that the memorandum was written, but that everything already announced its "inevitable triumph." It had been foreseen at the beginning of the French Revolution and subsequently had been deployed by "those sovereigns of sovereigns," the Rothschild brothers. The result, Allonville announced, was predictable.

Ever since Adam Smith said that "money is nothing other than the motive force (*mobile*) of circulation," it has come to be seen by economists as no more than a representative sign of wealth, with credit as real wealth, giving rise to the creation of fictive values equally representative of that same wealth. Hence, banks, paper-money, and speculation as the fruits of the abundance of public effects, culminating in the aristocracy of the Bourse and the endless resources of loans and debts or, more accurately, disguised bankruptcy, because the multiplication of the sign undermines its value, and the final result of that multiplication will probably be a great financial catastrophe.[3]

In the age of the Rothschilds, Allonville concluded, it was no longer public opinion that was queen of the world, but real or fictive money.

The initial claim of this essay is, therefore, that the concept of capitalism began as a concept that looked back to the eighteenth-century preoccupation with the nexus of capital, war, and debt but acquired its conceptual identity when that conceptual nexus was transferred from an international to

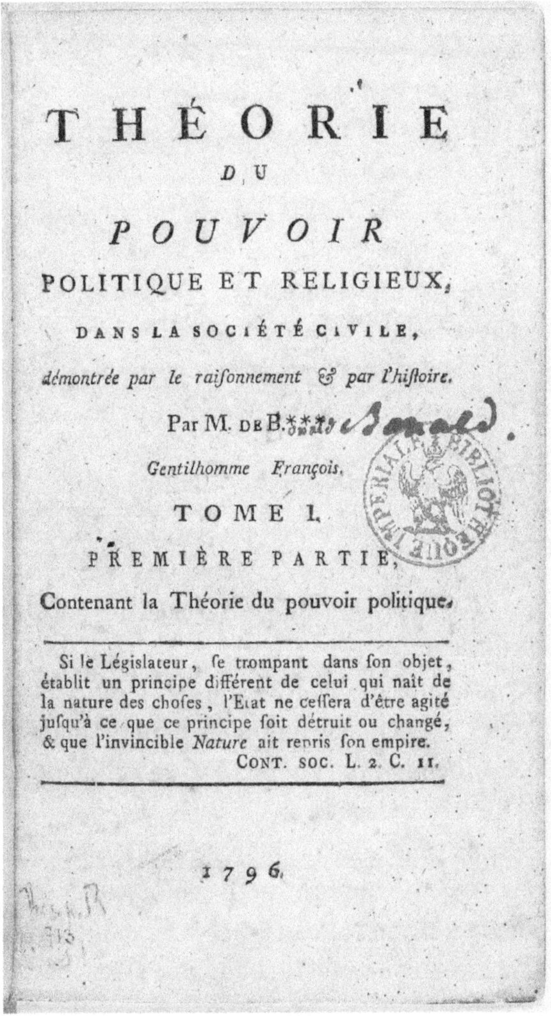

THÉORIE

DU

POUVOIR

POLITIQUE ET RELIGIEUX,

DANS LA SOCIÉTÉ CIVILE,

démontrée par le raisonnement & par l'histoire.

Par M. DE B*****. *Bonald*

Gentilhomme François.

TOME I.

PREMIÈRE PARTIE,

Contenant la Théorie du pouvoir politique.

Si le Législateur, se trompant dans son objet,
établit un principe différent de celui qui naît de
la nature des choses, l'État ne cessera d'être agité
jusqu'à ce que ce principe soit détruit ou changé,
& que l'invincible *Nature* ait repris son empire.
CONT. SOC. L. 2. C. 11.

1796.

FIGURE 4. Louis de Bonald, *Théorie du pouvoir politique et religieux dans la société civile* (1796)

a national setting. In this respect, it inherited much of its content from an older, still French, but largely royalist literature centred on Britain's rise to world power in the eighteenth century and the price that both Britain and the rest of the world had paid for it. In this literature, the concept of a commercial society was counterposed to the concept of a political society, but, in contradistinction to later usage, the combination was taken to be a harbinger of ruin rather than revolution. In this type of argument, the concept of a commercial society was, ultimately, self-defeating. This was the type of argument that was set out vividly in 1796 by the royalist political theorist Louis de Bonald in his *Théorie du pouvoir politique et religieux dans la société civile* (Theory of political and religious power in civil society), partly to explain why it would be a mistake for opponents of the French Revolution to advocate a mixed or British-style system of government as an alternative to the republican regime presently in power in France.

"In England," Bonald wrote, "there are two *powers* because there are two societies." There was a political society, which was constituted and monarchical, but there was also a commercial society (here Bonald used the term *une société de commerce*, which was the one used in the first, 1790, French translation of Adam Smith's *Wealth of Nations*). It was, he wrote, "the most extensive there has ever been in the universe because the state is commercial in England and is properly commercial only in England."[4]

In this commercial society, Bonald continued, power was separated by its nature from the power that existed in political society. There, power was unitary, while the power that existed in commercial society was collective. To explain the difference between the two types of power, Bonald drew upon a distinction between two types of society described much earlier by the seventeenth-century English political philosopher Thomas Hobbes. Some societies were bound together so tightly that they formed a union. Others, however, relied on reciprocity and concord.[5] To Bonald, a commercial society was one of these. Unlike a political society, a commercial society was not a society in which it was "the opposition of particular interests and opposing wills that made the establishment of that type of society necessary, but the free union of common interests and unanimous wills *that made it possible*."[6] On Bonald's terms, a commercial society was synonymous with concord, while a political society presup-posed union. The combination of the two, which, he argued, was a distinctively British attribute, was both a strength and, ultimately, a weakness. It would be a strength for as long as the commercial society left the executive with the initiative to maintain peace at home and project power abroad. But it would turn out to be a fatal weak-ness if government policy gave rise to financial instability and to arguments and conflict over taxation and public expenditure. Then, Bonald argued, fear of royal power would provoke the commercial society to encroach upon the politi-cal society; the resulting spiral of uncertainty and instability, which, he argued, was built into collec-tive decision making, would give rise to war, civil war, and, ultimately, catastrophic state failure. This, he claimed, was the real meaning of the enigmatic prophecy that Montesquieu had issued about Britain's future in 1748 in his *The Spirit of Laws*. "This state will perish," Montesquieu had written, "when the legislative power has become more corrupt than the executive."[7] France and the events of the French Revolution were, from Bon-ald's point of view, in the process of proving that Montesquieu had supplied the right answer even if he had singled out the wrong country. It was a characterisation of the French Revolution that had a striking resemblance to the one set out some two centuries later by the great German historian Reinhart Koselleck in his *Critique and Crisis*.[8]

In Bonald's rendition, a commercial society was condemned to fail because, in the final analysis, it did not have the stability supplied by the vertical structure of command that was the hallmark of a properly constituted political society. Much the same diagnosis applied to capitalism, but instead of the tensions between borderless trade and commercial reciprocity on the one hand and bounded politics and political authority on the other that were the hallmarks of Bonald's characterisation of commercial society, the tensions that first gave capitalism its name arose in the context of domestic struggles for power. As can be seen from Bonald's examination of Britain as a warning to France and from the compilation edited by Allonville, capitalism, like many other words that end in -ism, was used by writers from the royalist and legitimist right of French politics during the 1830s to crystallise both the problem and the challenge that could be generated by turning a single word into a signal of the moral

and political choices that France now faced.[9]
Much the same type of ideological crystallisation
lay behind the long list of potential causes of
French ruin set out by another royalist, Pons
Louis Frédéric, marquis de Villeneuve, in a pamphlet entitled *De l'agonie de la France* (France's
agony) published in 1839. As its title indicated, the
pamphlet was intended to highlight the many
threats to French survival built, according to Villeneuve, into the arrangements and policies followed by the July Monarchy, beginning with the
decline of Christianity, the inadequacies of education, the "pulverisation" of the soil and the
family by the "progressive solvent" of the Civil
Code, and the ruin of both the old and the new
aristocracy—whether noble or bourgeois, provided that they owned land—under the aegis of
the new "democratic element." The threat of ruin
extended to property owners because of the combination of inequality and a poorly timed land
tax; to industrialists because of the impoverish-
ment of the soil and the resulting potential for
"general disorganisation"; "to capitalism and finance" because of the oversupply of credit; to
rentiers because of the fiscal squeeze produced by
providing an income to "people who take but do

not give"; and, ultimately, to almost every component of modern French society. "Alongside the malaise or instability of private wealth," Villeneuve warned, "there is the complementary and more penetrating malaise of public wealth. A new evil, *capitalism*, that seductive and dangerous serpent, threatens to suffocate them both in its coils."[10]

It could be claimed, therefore, that the concept of capitalism began as either a French royalist nightmare or a royalist political threat. In this respect, its meaning was somewhat similar to that of the phrase "the social question" that also began to become current and also initially in legitimist circles in the decade after the French revolution of July 1830. The point of the phrase was made clear in an article published in November 1831 in a legitimist newspaper named *La Quotidienne* attacking the Orleanist regime for its failure to win a broad body of popular support after a major insurrection by silk workers in the city of Lyon. "In the end," the newspaper commented, "it is necessary to understand that, beyond the parliamentary conditions on which the existence of power depends, there is a social question that still has to be answered. . . . A government is always wrong if it has no more to offer than a flat refusal to listen to people calling for bread."[11] The social question, in this rendition, was a question about a government that was based on the idea of popular sovereignty, but refused to recognise the needs and entitlements of the sovereign author of its power. Ultimately, on these premises, the real answer to the social question would have to be a reforming (legitimist or Bonapartist) royal government.

V

Capitalism and the Right to Work

THE POLITICAL IMPLICATIONS of the social question were connected to the conceptual and political transformation that saw the subject of capitalism move from the French right to the French left. By 1847 a multivolume *Histoire de la classe ouvrière depuis l'esclave jusqu'au prolétaire de nos jours* written by a Christian and socialist named Joseph Robert, known as Robert du Var, could announce:

Rejoice, proletarian, your emancipation is at hand. It is sure and it is certain because you have come to know the cause and remedy of the misfortunes that have befallen you. Placed as you are above the factual by the ideal that you incarnate, you have come to know a higher life than the life that capitalism has made for you and still seeks to prolong. Proletarian, you are not simply a republican; you are a socialist, a socialist like Saint-Simon, Fourier, Robert Owen, Pierre Leroux, Louis Blanc, Proudhon and, like them, you understand human solidarity and association. You know how to reason of labour and capital and talk of science and art. You know the worth of humanity.[1]

This was the usage that meant that a term which, until then, had been used mainly in political commentary and in legitimist and royalist political propaganda became more like the concept of capitalism that was passed down from the nineteenth century.

The new meaning was registered very clearly in 1848 in a note added to a eulogy of a once-famous French philanthropist named Benjamin Delessert whose life and achievements as a sugar manufacturer, liberal politician, and philanthropist were the subject of a prize competition put on in 1846 by the Royal Academy of Science, Arts and Fine

Arts of his native city of Lyon. In his speech introducing the prize-winning entry, the secretary of the committee responsible for making the award made a point of highlighting the relationship between capital and philanthropy. "Capital," he asserted, "is the lever used by trade and industry to make the world turn around (*remouer*). Break that lever that is presently held in the hands of the rich; divide it among everyone; what would you be able to do with that atom of a lever, that drop of water from the immense sea which, once divided, would not be able to turn even a mill made of paper? Let it not be forgotten: wealth divided is universal poverty."[2] To reinforce the point, he inserted a note saying that there had, recently, been a struggle between the poet and politician Alphonse de Lamartine and the journalist and socialist Louis Blanc that, he wrote, had given rise to a new word: *capitalism*. "It is not on capital," the latter was said to have proclaimed, "that we have declared war, but on *capitalism*." But, to the supporter of philanthropy, Blanc's distinction was meaningless. Capitalism still called for capitalists.

This is something I can see perfectly well and we can all understand this. We can see that it is

not really capital that irritates you, but capitalists. But can Monsieur Louis Blanc tell us what
will become of capital without capitalists? It
will, I suppose, become what water becomes if
you take away the reservoir containing it.[3]

But there was, in fact, a significant distinction between capitalism and capitalists. Capitalists were
individuals who owned property, which, because
they owned it, was private property. Capitalism,
however, did not have to refer immediately or directly either to private property or to real individuals because, as Louis Blanc insisted, it was the name
of a system. It was this distinction that was really at
issue in the protracted public argument between
Louis Blanc and Alphonse de Lamartine.

The argument had, in fact, begun several years
earlier when, late in 1844, Lamartine published
what he called "a long article on political economy" in the periodical *Le Bien public*, which, at
that time, was something like his own house periodical. The article was entitled "Du droit au travail
et de l'organisation du travail" (On the right to
work and the organisation of work) and was a full-
blooded attack not only on Louis Blanc's famous
pamphlet, *Organisation du travail*, first published

in 1839, but also on what, in his private correspondence, Lamartine called an assortment of "com-
munists, Fourierists, etc.," who, like Louis Blanc,
had adopted the call for the right to work.[4] The
concept itself was introduced to public debate by
the strange early nineteenth-century French socialist Charles Fourier. "I have no wish," he announced in his *Theory of the Four Movements*, which
began to appear in 1822, "to start an argument
about those re-hashed Greek daydreams about the
rights of man, which have become so ridiculous.
After the revolutions that they caused we are now
heading for more troubles because we have forgotten the chief and only useful right among them,
the right to work."[5] By the 1830s, Fourier's new
concept had become a subject of a considerable
interest. Lamartine's aim was clearly to add a measure of critical intensity to this debate because he
made a point of sending the proofs of his pamphlet to the Parisian press magnate Emile de Girardin to ensure that it would be given as much
publicity as possible. Girardin passed it on to the
political economist Adolphe Blanqui while Lamartine sent another copy to the equally well-
known political economist Frédéric Bastiat. Bastiat published a critical comment on Lamartine's

pamphlet, as too, but with a different objective, did Blanc. The "new word," *capitalisme*, that was singled out at a prize-day ceremony in Lyon was therefore the product of a debate between Lamartine and his more forthright political-economist allies, Bastiat and Blanqui, on the one side and Blanc and his more forthright socialist allies, Victor Avril and Pierre Leroux, on the other.

The argument between the two sides began, therefore, long before the subject of the right to work became a live political issue with the revolution of February 1848. It continued even after the 1848 revolution ended with the election of Louis Napoleon Bonaparte to be president of the soon-to-be-terminated second French Republic. One measure of its scale and scope was a large two-volume compilation entitled *Le droit au travail* published by Lamartine's press ally Emile de Girardin in 1849. The scale and scope of the debate were a measure of the real analytical challenge to the idea of the right to work that Lamartine issued in his 1844 pamphlet. As he presented it, there was a radical contradiction between the concepts of the right to work and individual liberty. In practice, he argued, each could have a real existence only at the expense of the other. In this respect, Lamartine's treatment of the subject of the right to work was similar to Constant's treatment of negative and positive liberty. Where Constant took negative liberty to be a threat to positive liberty and called for some sort of unspecified combination of the two, Lamartine acknowledged that the absence of work gave rise to the call for the right to work, but, unlike Louis Blanc, rejected the claim that recognition of the right would in fact supply the work. Over time, the substance of the argument was largely forgotten; it is only relatively recently, notably in the work of Michel Foucault and his student François Ewald, that it has begun to be seen again as something fundamental to the intellectual history of the welfare state and, more broadly, to the intellectual foundations of both modern political thought and modern politics.[6]

Lamartine set out the problem built into the concept of the right to work very clearly. The initial problem with the concept, he wrote, was that it was a right and, like any other right, it was, by definition, enforceable. Unlike purely moral entitlements or social conventions, rights were legal and could be enforced by government, laws, and the state. "As for the organisation of labour," Lamartine wrote in 1844, "meaning some sort of sovereign intervention by the state in the relationship of workers to employers and capital to wages, an intervention in which the state regulates production and consumption and governs capital and wages, we have to confess that we do not have enough intelligence to rise up to an understanding of how a free government can be ruled by what is arbitrary and for monopoly to be the basis of free competition."[7] He then went on to spell out the implications of this impossible combination as a series of rhetorical questions.

> What do you mean, we need to ask, by *the organisation of labour*? Is it to be the reestablishment of exclusive guilds and workers' corporations, of *jurandes* and *maîtrises*, to form a set of legal cadres that only a certain number of workers would be allowed to enter for fear that any larger number would exceed the needs of the trade and begin to compete with one another? But it is not hard to see that by guaranteeing work for those inside the cadre, you will be denying it to those outside the cadre and ruin with one hand the work that you want to guarantee with the other. The French Revolution was

made so that every type of employment could be freely accessible to every citizen, but do you want now to begin by declaring that work and wages and our daily bread will be accessible to some and inaccessible to others? Having toppled the aristocracy and feudalism from the pinnacle of society, do you want to restore an aristocracy of labour and a feudalism of wages at the lowest levels of your social order? Having destroyed the nobility of ranks, do you want to create a nobility of tools? Having won civil and political liberty, do you now want to establish occupational slavery and arbitrariness? But this would be the most stupid of counterrevolutions! It would mean having two contradictory principles of government in the same state and cutting the nation in two. It amounts to declaring that what is true above is false below and that, while the political and property-owning part of the country will be ruled by liberty, the working and proletarian part will be ruled by what is arbitrary, meaning that there will be a nation of citizens and a nation of slaves. But what is the point of discussion? It is enough to challenge anyone who wants to achieve it to go about realising this suicide of liberty. If there is anyone foolish enough to try it, where is the people that is prepared to suffer it?[8]

But, for all its rhetorical power, Lamartine's attack on the concept of the right to work won few supporters, if only because he made it clear that his aim was to identify a position somewhere between free-market liberals like Bastiat and socialists like Blanc.

To Bastiat, Lamartine's attack on the concept of the right to work did not go far enough. Justice, he argued, was a clear and simple principle that states and their governments existed to maintain and enforce. This was, however, not the case with more nebulous principles like welfare, solidarity, or fraternity. "Fraternity," Bastiat wrote, "involves, by definition, making a sacrifice for someone else and working for someone else. This, when it is free, spontaneous, and voluntary, I can understand and applaud. The greater the sacrifice the more I am prepared to applaud. But if the principle of fraternity is to be imposed on society by law, meaning, in plain language, if the distribution of the fruits of labour is to be done by legislative means, with no consideration of the rights of labour itself, who is to say how far this principle will go; what form it will be given by legislative caprice; and in what institutions it would come to be incarnated by decrees made from one day to the next? Can a society even exist on these terms?"[9]

The argument that Bastiat used was an updated version of the old distinction between perfect and imperfect rights established in the tradition of modern natural jurisprudence in the seventeenth century by Hugo Grotius, Thomas Hobbes, and Samuel Pufendorf. Perfect rights, like those attached to contracts, property, or inheritance, could be enforced by law. Imperfect rights, like those associated with friendship, hospitality, or neighbourliness, were voluntary. As Bastiat presented it, the right to work was a right of the latter type. To rely on the state to secure and protect work in the way that it secured and protected property was, Bastiat asserted, a category mistake. Work and employment were, ultimately, matters of individual choice. Property, however, either existed or did not exist. Someone would still be the same person with or without work, but something would be a very different thing depending on whether or not it was owned. At most, the state's responsibility was to establish conditions that made as many choices and as much work available to as many of its members as possible.

As Bastiat recognised, Lamartine's position, despite their differences, was nearer to his own. The problem, for Lamartine, was that there did not seem to be a tenable position midway between Bastiat and Blanc, or between the old binary opposition between perfect and imperfect rights. As with the opposition between positive and negative liberty, there did not seem to be a position between individual contracts of employment and generalised legal rights. Opting for the first meant following Bastiat. Opting for the second meant following Blanc. Significantly, however, it was Blanc himself who began to show that a third position was possible, and that it was likely to be found by thinking more fully and clearly about the differences between capitalists and capitalism. Thus, although it is the case that the word "capitalism" was used intermittently quite independently of Blanc, there is still some reason to associate the concept of capitalism with Louis Blanc and, more specifically, with the substance of his argument with Lamartine.[10]

Blanc first used the term in a vigorous reply to Lamartine. "You reproach the socialists," he wrote in his periodical *Le Nouveau Monde* in 1849, "with wanting to suppress capital and capitalists. Idiocy (*Bêtise*)! What you are doing here is to conflate something that socialists would never conflate and which allows you to attribute your own ignorance to them. In any system, note this well, capital is absolutely indispensable to the work of agricultural or industrial production. But, far from losing its utility in passing from the service of an isolated individual to the service of an association, it actually magnifies it. By concentrating, far from perishing, capital actually grows. The suppression of *capitalism* has nothing to do with the suppression of *capital*. Is assembling the separate detachments of an army the same as destroying it?"[11] Capitalism, for Blanc, meant the private appropriation of capital. The solution, therefore, was to socialise or nationalise it. Capital was, therefore, the means to neutralise capitalism. National or social capital would have all the advantages of scale and scope that were unavailable to capital that was privately and individually owned. It could be raised in bulk, invested in bulk, to produce in bulk and, on the basis of this massive increase in output, could then be used to distribute in bulk. It would provide the means to turn many separate small-scale organisations into a smaller number of much larger vertically and horizontally integrated organisations. Capital without capitalism was production on a social scale and the promise of a different world. This was the reason for the title of Louis Blanc's periodical, *Le nouveau monde* (The new world), and its close similarity to the title of the Anglo-Welsh socialist Robert Owen's *The New Moral World*.

VI

Capitalism in a
Divided World

LOUIS BLANC'S DISTINCTION of capital and capitalists from capitalism as such makes it possible to
bring more precision to bear on the mixture of
continuity and discontinuity involved in the concepts of both capitalism and socialism as they came
to be formulated before and after the revolutions
of 1848. As Blanc described the two concepts, capitalism was a system in which capital was privately
owned, while socialism was one in which capital
was publicly owned. Although his version of socialism was not particularly different from other proposals to establish a new type of interrelationship
of capital, capitalism, and the division of labour, it

began to grow more prominent both because of Blanc's established reputation as the author of *The Organisation of Labour* and because of his strong endorsement of the relationship between the public ownership of capital and the concept of the right to work. It took some time for Blanc to establish his position. Although *The Organisation of Labour* was reprinted several times after its first publication in 1839, it was only after Blanc's confrontation with Lamartine that he began to make a strong distinction between capital and capitalism and call for the public ownership of capital as a simultaneous solution to the problem of capitalism and the problem of the right to work.

The proposal was an unusual mixture of the old and the new. Capitalism, at least as the term was used in the early 1830s, referred primarily to the eighteenth-century system of war finance, when states and their rulers borrowed large sums of money to fund the sudden, often massive increases in government expenditure caused by war or the threat of war. That practice continued to inform the early uses of the term "capitalism" in the first three decades of the nineteenth century when, as a number of historians have shown, defence expenditure continued to account for the largest share of state expenditure. In this sense, and until the fourth decade of the nineteenth century, public debt was usually seen as the other side of warfare. With Blanc, however, public debt became the other side of welfare. Intermittently, but substantially, the switch from warfare to welfare has become the hallmark of state expenditure ever since the age of Louis Blanc.

There was, however, an exception. In keeping with at least one significant line of eighteenth-century thought, using public debt to fund the switch from warfare to welfare was still compatible with this side of eighteenth-century usage. This assessment of the potential of public debt was made very early in the eighteenth century by the Scottish political economist and financier John Law in the elaborate scheme that he devised to use a combination of a public bank, a state-funded paper currency, and a huge trading company to generate a stream of income that was designed to lower interest rates and favour investment in agriculture, industry, and trade, with the longer-term result that their profitability could then be used to liquidate large swathes of private debt. According to Law, public debt could, paradoxically, generate private prosperity. Although Law's system failed catastrophically, the idea of turning public debt into an engine of growth had an enduring fascination. It was most visible in the eighteenth century in the thought of the Scottish Jacobite political economist Sir James Steuart and his many French followers in the early years of the French Revolution. It continued into the second and third decades of the nineteenth century when Law's ideas again began to be widely described and discussed, particularly in France before and after the revolution of July 1830. In this respect, Louis Blanc's idea of relying on capital, because it was publicly owned, to eliminate capitalism, because it was privately owned, was the direct descendant of Law's system.

In another, more important respect, however, Blanc's version of socialism was very different from eighteenth-century usage. This was because substituting capital for capitalism still had to address the problem of the right to work. The right to work was, certainly, connected to the subjects of capital and capitalism, but it was also connected to the division of labour. But the division of labour was not necessarily a local or even a national problem because it was also international or global. In this context, Lamartine and even

Bastiat had a point. Making the right to work a real right, a right that was perfect in the old, seventeenth-century sense of the term because it was a right that would be enforced by the law and the state, amounted to imposing an intrinsically undefinable constraint not only on the myriads of occupations and activities within any single economy but also on the structure, composition, and viability of every economy in an economically divided world. Establishing and maintaining the right to work under these conditions could mean, very literally, turning socialism into national socialism. With this as its possible outcome it is not clear, as Lamartine insisted vociferously, whether the right to work was a promise or a threat.

The real problem, as should now be clear, was not capital or capitalism, but the division of labour. There were many possible alternatives to capitalism, some more viable than others, but the range of alternatives to the division of labour is not all that easy to see. In part this is because the solutions to the two problems are different. As Louis Blanc presented it, dealing with the problem of capitalism called for centralising the ownership of capital. Instead of the many different owners of capital responsible for the existence of capitalism, there could be a single, state-based, owner of capital that would be responsible for welfare just as eighteenth-century states like Britain had been responsible for warfare. But the problem of the division of labour was a different type of problem. Here, centralisation was as likely to magnify as to eliminate the problem, not only because of the difficulties involved in identifying and allocating resources and activities within any particular economy, but also because any local and particular set of choices and decisions would be subject to the consequences of many other, less controllable but equally local, choices and decisions. Ownership is simple and binary, but decision making is complicated and multidimensional because it usually involves comparisons between things separated by time and space. Solutions to the problem of capitalism are, therefore, not necessarily solutions to the problem of the division of labour. There are, therefore, good analytical and historical reasons to think that Adam Smith had something quite precise in mind in giving the name "commercial society" to the type of society that came after hunting, pastoral, and agricultural societies.

The significance of the distinction between capitalism and commercial society is also relevant to the problem of putative solutions. Here, the dilemma that Lamartine was one of the first to highlight is still salient. If the nationalisation of capital was a solution to the problem of capitalism but did not have much purchase on the problem of the division of labour, while establishing the right to work was a solution to the problem of the division of labour but did not have much purchase on the problem of capitalism, it begins to look as if something different would have to be found. If, in the second place, the problem of capital began as a problem of war and, in this guise, was as familiar in Adam Smith's day as the problem of the division of labour had become by the time that it was addressed by Lamartine and Louis Blanc, then there is good reason to think that, before they were conflated under the broad and misleading rubric of capitalism, the two problems were once discussed separately. There is, in other words, good reason to think that the first step towards clarifying the problem of capitalism is to start with two problems rather than one. Starting with two problems also means thinking about two solutions rather than one, a

solution to the problem of capital and the ownership of capital in the first place and, in the second
place, a different solution to the problem of the
division of labour and markets. The aim of the second part of this essay is to begin to describe what
these were. Here too, the starting point was supplied by Adam Smith because, as several of Smith's
later readers went to some lengths to point out,
Smith's concept of political economy was based on
both a theory of justice on the one hand and, on
the other, a theory of expediency. Together, they
amounted to a new and different approach to the
subject of politics in commercial society.

PART II

Solutions

VII

Karl Marx—Capitalism, Communism, and the Division of Labour

ONCE, THE BEST-KNOWN ALTERNATIVE to capitalism was communism. It is less clear, however, that communism was an equivalent alternative to a commercial society. This is why it is worth beginning with communism before describing the earlier discussions of the problematic quality of a commercial society. Starting with communism makes it easier to see what, in relation to capitalism, communism was designed to solve and what, by contrast, the various participants in the earlier discussions of commercial society took to be the problems that *they* had to solve. For Marx, in contradistinction to these earlier writers, the fundamental problem was the problem of property and, more specifically, the peculiar type of property that Marx called labour-power. On this basis, the ultimate solution to the problem of property and, particularly, property in labour-power was to be supplied by the division of labour. For almost everyone else, however, the relationship between the problem and the solution was the other way round. Here, the fundamental problem was the division of labour, while the solutions to the problem were expected, instead, to come from different types of property.

It was once usual to say that communism was a kind of synthesis of British political economy, German philosophy, and French socialism. The claim was made initially by Marx and Engels themselves and has continued to echo down the ages. It would be more accurate, however, to say that communism was a kind of synthesis of French legal thought and German theology as these developed between 1830 and 1848, partly in opposition to British political economy and its French followers including, most famously, Jean-Baptiste Say. This was because French legal thought and

German theology contained two concepts that were central to Marx's concept of communism. The first was the idea of a negative community of goods, while the second was the idea of individual autonomy. Together, as Marx used them, they appeared to offer the prospect of a solution to the combined problems of property and the division of labour.

The concept of a negative community of goods is now known only to specialists in legal history and among some students of Marxism.[1] It was, however, still alive in the United States at the very end of the nineteenth century where it was used in the context of a Supreme Court ruling on whether the state of Connecticut was entitled to prohibit the export of game birds beyond its borders even though the killing of game birds was authorised and allowed within its borders. It also had a prominent presence in eighteenth-century English jurisprudence, this time in the context of the English Game Laws and, more specifically, the treatment of the right to hunt by the English jurist William Blackstone in his famous *Commentaries on the Laws of England*. The subject of property was central to the arguments laid out in both these settings because both sets of arguments turned on the related questions of whether wild animals could be legitimately owned and, by extension, of how it was possible to distinguish legal ownership from legitimate use.

The concept of a negative community of goods was designed, in the first place, to provide a way to distinguish ownership from use. It was originally a Roman law concept that, like much other Roman law, was incorporated into the great treatises of natural jurisprudence published in the seventeenth century by Hugo Grotius and Samuel Pufendorf. From Pufendorf, the concept was transmitted to a widely used eighteenth-century French treatise on property law written by a jurist named Robert Joseph Pothier, and from there it passed into the arguments addressed by the United States Supreme Court in 1895. "The first of mankind," Pothier wrote in his treatise on property in 1762,

had in common all those things which God had given to the human race. This community was not a positive community of interest, like that which exists between several persons who have the ownership of a thing in which each has his particular portion. It was a community which those who have written on the subject have called a negative community, which resulted from the fact that those things which were common to all belonged no more to one than to the others, and hence no one could prevent another from taking of these common things that portion which he judged necessary in order to subserve his wants. Whilst he was using them others could not disturb him, but when he had ceased to use them, if they were not things which were consumed by the fact of use, the things immediately re-entered into the negative community and another could use them. The human race having multiplied, men partitioned among themselves the earth and the greater part of those things which were on its surface. That which fell to each one among them commenced to belong to him in private ownership and this process is the origin of the right of property. Some things, however, did not enter into this division and remain therefore to this day in the condition of the ancient and negative community.[2]

The concept could still be found in the political philosopher Karl Salomon Zacharia's *Vierzig*

Bücher vom Staat (Forty books on the state) of 1843 and in the German political economist Wilhelm Roscher's *Principles of Political Economy* of 1854, but it was given far more prominence by its appearance in Pierre Joseph Proudhon's explosive *Qu'est-ce qu'est la propriété?* (What is property?) of 1840. Property, Proudhon famously announced, was theft, and it was the concept of negative community that enabled him to say so.

The assertion was a straightforward reply to Pothier's assertion that God, having sovereign dominion over the universe and all the things within it, had created the earth and all its creatures for the benefit of humanity and had given humanity a dominion subordinate to his own.[3] This, Pothier had explained, was why the original community of goods given by God was a negative, not a positive, community. In it, nothing belonged to anyone because everything was available to everyone. It followed entirely logically, Proudhon pointed out, that property was theft, because property that was positively owned, even by the whole human race at any particular moment of time, must have been appropriated from the original negative community. Individual ownership was, therefore, appropriation on a compound scale. It had happened,

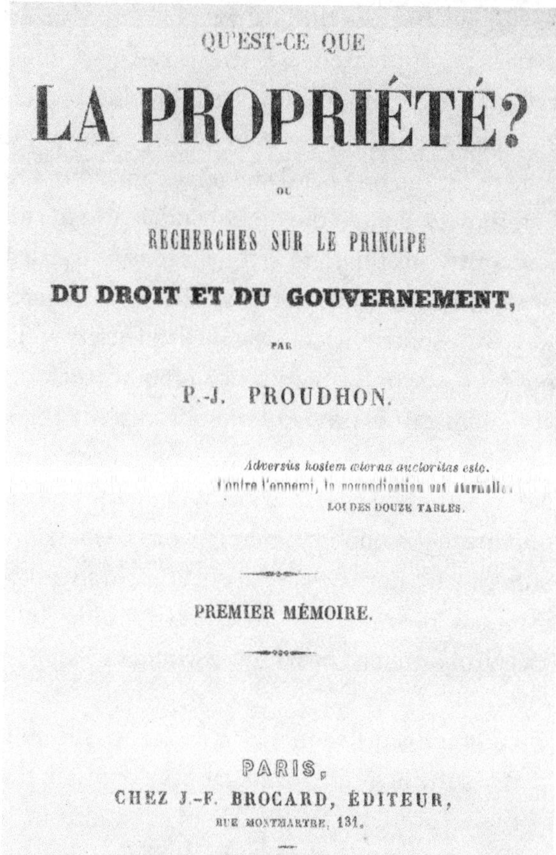

QU'EST-CE QUE

LA PROPRIÉTÉ?

OU

RECHERCHES SUR LE PRINCIPE

DU DROIT ET DU GOUVERNEMENT,

PAR

P.-J. PROUDHON.

Adversús hostem æterna auctoritas esto.
Contre l'ennemi, la revendication est éternelle.
LOI DES DOUZE TABLES.

PREMIER MÉMOIRE.

PARIS,
CHEZ J.-F. BROCARD, ÉDITEUR,
RUE MONTMARTRE, 131.

1840.

FIGURE 5. Pierre Joseph Proudhon,
Qu'est ce que la propriété? (1840)

he argued, because the abstract concept of property had supplanted the real use of particular things. For Proudhon, however, individual ownership also carried the seeds of its own solution. It meant, on the one hand, emancipation from the community, but, on the other hand, it also meant insecurity, isolation, and a struggle for survival that property alone could not solve. There had, therefore, to be something that was neither society without property, or the negative community that was communism, nor property without society, or egoism. Proudhon called it anarchy. It meant establishing social arrangements in terms of internal moral qualities, like honesty, courage, or compassion, rather than external material qualities, like wealth, ostentation, or display. "To express this idea by a Hegelian formula," he wrote, "I would say":

communism, first mode, first cause of sociability, is the first term of social development, the thesis; property, the reverse of communism, is the second term, the antithesis. When we have discovered the third term, the synthesis, we shall have the required solution. Now this synthesis necessarily results from the correction of the thesis by the antithesis; and so it is necessary, by a final examination of their characteristics, to eliminate those features which are hostile to sociability. The union of the two remainders will give us the true mode of humanitarian association."[4]

Communism, Proudhon continued, "rejects independence and proportionality," but property "satisfies neither equality nor law."[5] Building these four elements into social arrangements would make it possible to go beyond either the absence of property that came with the negative community or the absence of community that came with the presence of property. With equality and law based on possession and use, individual abilities in all their richness and diversity would, finally, have a home in human affairs.

With Proudhon, the concept of a negative community belonged to the past. With Marx, however, it belonged to the future. This, in part, was because his concept of the proletariat relied on a more positive evaluation of the division of labour than Proudhon was either willing or able to make. In this concept of the proletariat, the proletariat was the class responsible both for producing the wealth of the world and, ultimately, for

emancipating the world by making its own collective labour-power the source of a new, postcapi-
talist version of a negative community.[6] In part,
however, it was also because Marx's concept of
the proletariat as the source of a new version of a
negative community relied on two features of
early nineteenth-century German philosophy
that Proudhon himself did not know. The first was
a concept of the division of labour as a humanly
created analogue of the Creation itself. The second was a concept of collective action as *praxis* or
something more like the reflection, deliberation,
and choice usually associated with individual action because, unlike a collectivity, individuals are
usually taken to be persons, equipped with something called personality, or the ability to do things
voluntarily rather than involuntarily. Class consciousness, as Marx conceived it, was a product of
the proletariat's capacity to acquire or inject the
attributes of personality into the otherwise alien-
ated properties of labour-power.

This capacity was partly a product of the interdependence involved in the division of labour.
Since the proletariat had no property of its own, it
had to rely on work and wages in order to survive,
or, without work or wages on a general scale, it

would be forced to seize control of the means of production to provide itself with the means to live. Revolution, in this rendition, would preserve life, not property, and, since this was its goal, the real content of a modern revolution would be the creation of the conditions that were required to establish a genuinely negative community of goods. This time, however, it would be a community that owed more to culture than to nature and was grounded upon civilisation and science rather than kinship and custom. Communism, like the original negative community, would be based on the absence of ownership rather than on common ownership. It would bring back use instead of property and, in doing so, would break the chain binding individual needs to government, laws, and the state. Marx, it should be emphasised, was consistently hostile to the idea of equality. This was not because of any initial assumptions about superiority or inferiority, but instead because equality presupposed comparisons, relationships, and rules, while human needs, in the most literal of senses, were purely individual in character.

The source of this insistence on individuality was a Protestant theological tradition that had been picked up and used as the basis of a more secular philosophy of history by one of Marx's contemporaries, Ludwig Feuerbach. Its starting point was the question of why the Creation was required, or could have been necessary at all. God, after all, was perfect in every way, and it was not easy to explain why something equipped with every possible power should have wished to add to perfection itself. One answer was that the one thing that it was not possible for God to do was to create another divinity, because it would, self-evidently, be indistinguishable from the existing God. The point of creating was, after all, something created. In keeping with the logic of this argument, this was why the point of the Creation was humanity. Although God could not create another God, God could, nonetheless, create humanity, and if every human could develop and express his and her individual abilities and qualities as comprehensively as they could, then God would have created something like another divinity without actually having created another God.

The idea circulated initially in the late eighteenth- and early nineteenth-century romantic, but also theological, circles associated with the young Hegel and Friedrich Schelling. Over the course of the nineteenth century, it turned into one of the key components of the sociology of Georg Simmel and, later, into one of the foundational concepts of the differentiation theory of the twentieth-century German sociologist Niklas Luhmann.[7] One of its main targets was the philosopher Immanuel Kant, while one of its most eloquent exponents was the Protestant theologian Friedrich Schleiermacher. The insight into the real significance of human diversity that accompanied this version of the idea of the Creation, Schleiermacher wrote in his *Monologen* of 1800, had become his "highest intuition." Before he had come to know it, he explained, he had subscribed simply to the conventional view that "humanity revealed itself as varied only in the manifold diversity of outward acts," and that individuals were not, as he put it, "uniquely fashioned" but were, instead, fundamentally "one substance and everywhere the same." The new insight entailed a radical change of perspective. Instead of each individual coming to represent the generic attributes of humanity, each individual would come, uniquely, to represent him- or herself. "I saw clearly," Schleiermacher wrote, "that each man is meant to represent humanity in his own way, combining its elements uniquely, so that it may reveal itself in every mode and that all that can issue from its womb can be made actual in the fullness of unending space and time."[8] From this perspective, the division of labour could be redescribed as something that was considerably more than it seemed. Humanity, taken as a whole and if it was equipped with all the capabilities of its individual members, would have the potential to rise to the omnicompetence of the divinity. Appearances notwithstanding, there was a point to the division of labour that transcended work and wages or any type or form of property. Human society could display all the attributes of the divinity if it could reach the right level of diversity coupled with the right level of integration. As Ludwig Feuerbach wrote in his *Essence of Christianity*, "the true sense of theology is anthropology and there is no distinction between the *predicates* of the divine and human nature, and, consequently, no distinction between the divine and human *subject*."[9]

On this basis, the division of labour could be seen as a bridge between causality and creativity, or as the link that connected the phenomenal world of natural causation to the noumenal world of divine creation. As another of Marx's contemporaries, an unusual Polish philosopher and theologian named August Cieszkowski, began to show, the division of labour could now be understood as the key to the realisation of what Feuerbach described as an identity of predicates.[10] Here, the idea of humanity as something capable of matching the omnicompetence of the divinity was reinforced by the further thought that, in one crucial respect, humanity was equipped with a resource that God did not actually need. This was a knowledge of space and time. God, being eternal, transcended space and time. Humans, being finite, inhabited space and time. If humanity could find a way to use space and time to combine diversity with integration, then these two measures of human finitude could become the medium that enabled humanity to acquire the attributes of personality and, in a real sense, become like a God. To do so, humanity would have to find a way to build something like the reflexive capability used by individuals in making their choices and decisions into its own much more comprehensive culture and consciousness. Cieszkowski gave the name of *praxis* to this capacity for collective consciousness and collective action. Like many other people of his generation, he went on to show how it was history, meaning both people and events in the past *and* the subsequent understanding of people and events in the past, that had the power to turn individual consciousness into collective consciousness and individual choice into social *praxis*.

There were several other conceptual contributions to the philosophy of history that formed the basis of *The Communist Manifesto* and its terse initial announcement that the history of "all hitherto existing society" was the history of class struggles.[11] But the philosophy of history that gave *The Communist Manifesto* its content and direction was a philosophy of history that had property at its centre and its core. It began with the appropriation of goods from nature. It continued with the expropriation of goods that were originally possessed and then went on to follow the forcible transformation of possession into property, of users into owners, and of the dispossessed into sellers of labour-power as, slowly and violently, the social and economic arrangements of a world made up of the two great classes of bourgeois and proletarians came comprehensively into view. Increasingly, the contradictions between the freedom of the market and the despotism of the factory, and between the circulation of commodities and the consumption of labour-power would, the *Communist Manifesto* predicted, give rise cumulatively to an insuperable tension between the ownership of capital and the needs of the proletariat. Conflict would be followed by conflict, and the history of that conflict would be registered as class consciousness. This was why, in the final analysis, the expropriators would be expropriated, and the class that owned no property would turn a world that belonged to the bourgeoisie into a world that had really been made by the proletariat and which was now available for its use. In keeping with the argument of Marx's theses on Feuerbach, *The Communist Manifesto* turned the story of the Creation into a story about how the division of labour would turn, by way of collective *praxis*, into a negative community based on need and use.

But if need and use were the hallmarks of the new version of communism, where did this leave the division of labour? Capitalism would have gone because there would be no more property. But without the division of labour, what would remain? The government of men might well, as the phrase went, have been replaced by the administration of things, but the second part of the phrase could still raise as many questions as the first. Capitalism, in short, could well give rise to a world beyond property, but it is less easy to imagine a world beyond a commercial society. In this respect, the name itself is a clue to the thing. The main attribute of the thing, at least on Adam Smith's assessment, was that it was a society and not simply property. This is why the distinction between capitalism and a commercial society is still historically and analytically significant. To begin with Marx and the concept of capitalism is, therefore, to begin in midstream. Before Marx and before capitalism, the concepts and the reality of commercial society and the division of labour both existed, together with a large and partly forgotten body of discussion of how they had come to work and, from time to time, how they could be made to work differently.

Although the starting point of these discussions was supplied by Adam Smith and the concept of commercial society, there were also a number of other and further versions of what was involved in thinking about markets, politics, and the division of labour that were published before the concept of a commercial society was swallowed up by the concept of capitalism. Some, echoing Smith, involved examining the division of labour in terms of the relationship between justice and expediency, with the aim here of explaining how both could be accommodated by a single political system. Some authors, like Georg Wilhelm Friedrich Hegel, approached the subject of the division of labour from the vantage point of the relationship between civil society and the state, with the aim in this case of showing how an administrative system could straddle them both. Others, like David Ricardo, approached the subject of the division of labour from the perspective of international trade and comparative advantage, with the aim in this further case of explaining why a paper currency favoured commercial reciprocity. Yet others, like Lorenz von Stein after the revolutions of 1848, approached the subjects of civil society and the division of labour in terms of public debt and public administration, and began to call the outcome social democracy. The aim of what follows is to begin to piece these discussions together quickly and somewhat schematically because they help, cumulatively, to throw more light on capitalism than seems to have been possible by relying on the concept of capitalism itself.

VIII

Adam Smith— Capitalism, Utility, and Justice

THE ADAM SMITH PROBLEM, as it came to be called in Germany nearly a century after Adam Smith's death, was a German-language version of the earlier French discussion of the relationship between positive and negative liberty on the one side and between work and the right to work on the other. As was the case in the French discussion, the problem centred on the rival claims of individualism versus altruism under conditions of what, by then, was called, unequivocally, capitalism. The problem was encapsulated by the apparent discrepancy between the moral theory that Smith had set out in his *Theory of Moral Sentiments* of 1759 and the market theory set out in the *Wealth of Nations* in 1776. According to Smith's later critics, the basis of the moral theory was sympathy, while the basis of the market theory was self-interest. The Adam Smith Problem was whether—or how—the one could be reconciled with the other. The problem was first highlighted by the Swiss-German historian August Oncken in an article entitled "The Consistency of Adam Smith" that was published in 1897. It was followed, a year later, by the article in which Oncken gave the problem its official name as "Das Adam Smith–Problem."[1]

As Oncken explained in the earlier article, it had not been his aim to create the problem because it had already been given its existence, if not its name, in a number of earlier, mainly German-language, commentaries on Smith's work. These commentaries were largely the work of the German *Kathedersozialisten* (socialist academics) Bruno Hildebrand, Karl Knies, and Lujo Brentano, whose publications appeared after 1848 chiefly with the aim of giving political economy the kind of moral and social foundations that

Smith seemed initially to have recognised but then seemed to have abandoned. In this respect, the publications of the *Kathedersozialisten* paralleled the earlier French discussions of socialism, capitalism, and the right to work because, like them, they highlighted the role of the state in responding to market failures and in using its legal, fiscal, or financial powers to correct economic and social injustice. There was, therefore, a substantial overlap between the ideas of the German *Kathedersozialisten* and those of Louis Blanc, and a corresponding emphasis on state finance as an important part of any potential solution to the problem of capitalism. One effect of this late nineteenth-century preoccupation with socialism, the social question, and the right to work was that, by the end of the century, Smith's examination of the relationship of the division of labour to commercial society had been incorporated into a somewhat different examination of the relationship of capitalism to the state.

Oncken's formulation of the Adam Smith Problem has dominated discussions of the relationship between Smith's moral theory and his political economy from the late nineteenth century into the early twenty-first century.[2] Over time, it has grown

in scale and scope to encompass the broader subject of Smith's concept of justice and the question
of whether his theory was an anticipation of the
theory of justice developed by the late twentieth-
century Harvard philosopher John Rawls or, instead, was an echo of the earlier set of distinctions
made in the seventeenth century by the founder of
modern natural jurisprudence, Hugo Grotius, between perfect and imperfect rights and, by extension, between strict justice and a range of more
flexible and less binding moral obligations associated with utility, expediency, and virtue.[3] To his
contemporaries, however, Smith's theory
amounted to a more complicated system that was
designed to show how perfect and imperfect rights
could be combined with both justice and expediency. This was how Smith's system was described
by the philosopher Dugald Stewart in his *Account
of the Life and Writings of Adam Smith*, a memoir
that was published in 1793, two years after Smith's
death. According to Stewart, quoting the recollec-
tions of Smith's former, and then most famous,
student John Millar, Smith's treatment of the subject of justice in his Glasgow University lectures on
moral philosophy "followed the plan that seems to
be suggested by Montesquieu; endeavouring to

trace the gradual progress of jurisprudence, both public and private, from the rudest to the most refined ages, and to point out the effects of those arts which contribute to subsistence and to the accumulation of property, in producing correspondent improvements or alterations in law and government." Smith's aim, Stewart added, had been to publish this account of the development of laws and government, but his death in 1791 had meant that only the last part of the course, centred on "those political regulations which are founded, not upon the principle of *justice*, but that of *expediency*, and which are calculated to increase the riches, the power and the prosperity of a state," had seen the light of day.[4]

The published part of Smith's system, or the part "founded, not upon the principle of *justice*, but that of *expediency*," was the *Wealth of Nations*. The unpublished part was foreshadowed in the conclusion to the sixth edition of the *Theory of Moral Sentiments*, published in 1790. The problem was to try to work out how the two parts were connected. An initial indication of what the connection could have been began to appear a generation later in 1831 in a work entitled *A General View of the Progress of Ethical Philosophy* that was

published by another Scottish philosopher and
political theorist named Sir James Mackintosh.
Mackintosh (who died the following year) was a
member of the group of early nineteenth-century
Swiss and French moral, political, and economic
theorists associated with Benjamin Constant and
Germaine de Staël that has come to be known
as the Coppet group. He had in fact known Constant since the time when they were both students
at the University of Edinburgh in the 1780s; he
also became the brother-in-law of Constant's
close friend, the Franco-Swiss political economist
Jean Charles Léonard Simonde de Sismondi,
when they each married one of the three Allen
sisters (the third sister married one of Josiah
Wedgwood's sons) towards the end of the eighteenth century. Through Mackintosh, the distinction between negative and positive liberty that
was one of the hallmarks of the thought of the
Coppet group came to be associated with Smith's
distinction between expediency and justice.

Mackintosh made a point in his *General View
of the Progress of Ethical Philosophy* of highlighting
the dualism of Smith's system. Previous moral
theorists, he wrote, had not been sufficiently clear
in differentiating between what he called "two

perfectly distinct subjects: 1. The nature of the distinction between right and wrong in human conduct, and 2. The nature of those feelings with which right and wrong are contemplated by human beings."[5] Although they were both connected to the subject of justice, the first distinction was rational and analytical, while the second was emotional and relied on feelings of approval or disapproval. The emotional distinction, Mackintosh continued, gesturing towards Smith, had been called the "theory of moral sentiments," while the rational distinction between right and wrong involved examining the criteria of morality themselves. It was important, Mackintosh emphasised, to understand the difference between the two types of evaluation. Without this difference, it was easy to conflate justice with expediency by asserting, as the Anglican theologian and philosopher William Paley had done, that the principle of a moral sense was opposed to the principle of utility, as if the two principles referred to the same object. A moral sense, however, was something that approved of what was right and condemned what was wrong because it could identify something about the qualities of an action. The concept of utility, on the other hand, was a claim about the consequences of an action rather than about whether the action itself was right or wrong. "As these affirmations relate to different subjects," Mackintosh concluded, "they cannot be opposed to each other any more than the solidity of earth is inconsistent with the fluidity of water and a very little reflection will show it to be easily conceivable that they may both be true."[6] People could, spontaneously, approve or disapprove of certain actions on the basis of their feelings, but they could also use their reason to claim that the consequences of those actions were compatible or incompatible with general happiness or well-being.

There was, in short, no Adam Smith Problem because the theory of justice outlined in *The Theory of Moral Sentiments* could coexist readily with the theory of expediency underlying the *Wealth of Nations*. This, however, still left the problem of trying to work out how Smith thought that they actually could coexist without collapsing into each other. One attempt to do so was published a few years after Mackintosh's *General View of the Progress of Ethical Philosophy*. This was a book by another Scottish lawyer, this time named James Reddie, entitled *Inquiries Elementary and Historical in the Science of Law* that was first published in 1840 and then in a much larger second edition in 1847. The later version of the book had two main features. The first was its endorsement of Mackintosh's description of Smith's system as a combination of justice and expediency. The second feature of the book was Reddie's claim that Smith's theory of justice was the same as Immanuel Kant's. In both respects, Reddie drew out the implications of Smith's dualism. Justice, he argued, would sometimes have to trump expediency. Most of the time, however, expediency would be enough.

Reddie's description singled out two aspects of Smith's theory of justice. The first was the difference between justice and the other virtues. While the other virtues were usually recognised as virtues because of their freely chosen and voluntary character (liberality at gunpoint, for example, is usually described as robbery), the same voluntary character did not apply to justice. Justice, Smith had emphasised, was the only virtue that would retain its character even if it was backed up by force, usually in the form of the power and authority of the state. This was why justice was not quite the same as the other virtues. Although it could be an attribute of a person or a quality of an individual, it could also be as readily described as the quality of a relationship or the property of a system. Justice, in short, had as much to do with the rule of law and the concept of a legal system as with the actions and behaviour of individuals, peoples, or nations. This, in the second place, meant that justice could be associated with two, radically different, types of evaluation. One set of evaluations applied to human actions and the feelings of approbation or disapprobation involved in assessments of their possible causes, motives, or effects. Another set of evaluations, however, applied to human behaviour and the more rational range of assessments of the various possible consequences of different types of behaviour. Smith's use of the distinction, one that Reddie echoed, was a variation on the old Roman and Ciceronian distinction between the *honestum*, or honourable, and the *utile*, or useful.[7] Human actions could be subject to either type of evaluation, and this in turn meant that the evaluations themselves would differ. One would centre on justice itself, but the other would centre on consequences and the related concepts of expediency or utility. To Reddie, the most obvious example of how the distinction could work was in a market society. Here, face-to-face transactions did not usually have to occur. But there would still be rules and procedures, and their violation could still have consequences. In this case, however, the consequences would not necessarily be backed up by legal sanctions because questions of utility could apply to commercial relationships that stretched beyond the boundaries of any single state or legal system. The concept of justice was, in short, something that was likely to exist in several different ways. It could exist with or without a state and could be associated either with what was honourable or with what was useful. It was a product of rules but was also a product of judgement.

Reddie was not slow to point out the implications of this interpretation of Smith's system. "Indeed, in one vast department of human affairs," he wrote, "the principle of general expediency is the chief and almost the only moral criterion to which recourse can be had. In the complex details of political arrangement, in the intercourse of nations, the moral feeling which serves as a rule of conduct to the individual, although not silent, speaks with a comparatively feeble voice. We are led by a sort of moral impulse to perform the various duties of private life, but this guide in a great measure deserts us when we investigate the legislative, executive, judicial and economical establishments of civil society or the reciprocal transactions of independent states."[8] The theory of utility (or expediency) was not an alternative to a virtue-oriented theory of justice. They were instead different aspects of the same thing, and, as Reddie pointed out, both, in their different ways and in their different settings, were true. "While," he wrote, "with an Epicurus, a Hume or a Bentham," we can calculate pains and pleasures, we could also "with a Plato, a Marcus Aurelius, or a Seneca, with a Fénelon, a Shaftesbury, a Smith or a Brown" show "an ardent love and admiration of that incorruptible integrity, that disinterested and generous beneficence, that devoted and enlightened patriotism which are maintained and pursued solely as the right and becoming exercise by man of the powers delegated to him by his all-perfect creator."[9] The two were complementary, not incompatible.

Law, Reddie wrote in the second edition of his book, could be considered as a branch of morality that was centred on the virtue of justice. But if this was the case, law was a rather special branch of morality because its precepts operated "under the marked distinction (which Dr Adam Smith, it is believed, first pointed out in this country) that its rules are susceptible of enforcement, whereas compulsion is quite inconsistent with and even repugnant to the nature of the other virtues and would be destructive of their moral value."[10] In this respect, the law was not concerned with human arrangements and institutions as these were usually understood in rational or moral terms, but was concerned instead with humans "as sentient beings, dependent for their subsistence, clothing and shelter on their labour and on the produce of the earth, natural and industrial." In this sense, the law was a body of rules arising from "circumstances, necessity or urgent general expediency" and for "the safety, security and welfare of each individual and for the prosperity of the whole of these individuals united into one community." It relied for its enforcement on "the united strength of the community concentrated in the state or government," and this collective capacity was, in turn, put into effect "not so much by appealing to moral sentiment and the benevolent feelings of our nature as by operating, directly or indirectly, corporeally and mentally, upon the selfish feelings and the regard which every individual has for his own safety and welfare."[11] On these terms, the law existed to safeguard human choice.

Here, alongside Smith, Reddie now signalled Immanuel Kant as the prime source of this identification of the law with expediency. This view of law "as separate and distinct from, and independent of, morality," he wrote, "seems in modern times to have been first prominently brought forward by the German philosopher Kant, though perhaps it is only a more full development of the *necessitas* or *ratio juris* of the Roman Law."[12] This further identification of Kant with Roman law also had the effect of bringing Kant's moral and political thought into alignment with the thought of the early nineteenth-century German law professor Friedrich Carl von Savigny and the German historical school of law. As August Oncken was later to point out, it also helped to explain the hostility of the German *Kathedersozialisten* and the German historical school of economics towards the thought of both Kant and Smith. As Reddie emphasised, particularly in the second edition of his book, much of his own legal thinking owed a great deal to Savigny. This applied as much to Savigny's use of Kant as it did to the substance of Savigny's own legal thought. Both could be aligned with Smith and his distinction between justice as compulsory and binding and expediency as voluntary and discretionary. Together, as both Smith and Kant had shown, the two parts of the system made it possible for the power of the state to offset the power of the market.

To explain what Smith, Kant, and Savigny had in common, Reddie quoted a long passage from the first volume of Savigny's *System of Modern Roman Law* in which the German law professor had described the law as something that established "an invisible line of demarcation" which enabled each individual to enjoy "a secure and free space" as the basis of their dealings with others. The image revealed both the connection and the difference between the law and morality. "Law," Savigny wrote, "is subservient to morality, not because it accomplishes its precepts, but because its power secures to every individual the exercise and exhibition of his free will."[13] It was, therefore, a kind of carapace that allowed morality to function in much the same sense as it did with Kant's concept of autonomy, where autonomy was something that could coexist with a powerful royal sovereign. This, Savigny continued, meant that there was no contradiction if the continued existence of the law maintained "the immoral exercise" of a right that had been previously recognised as an actual right because, he explained, "the existence of law is a consequence of the imperfection of our condition: not an accidental historical imperfection, but such an one as is inseparably connected with the present stage of our existence." This idea too was very compatible with Kant's historical vision. Old laws might secure obsolete rights, but, to Savigny, obsolete rights could be allowed to fall away without further legislative coercion.

From this perspective, the law functioned as a kind of protective shield that covered individual and social development. It was consequently more than a simple remedy for injustice and more than a weapon to be used to right a wrong. As Savigny had emphasised, those who opted for this latter approach to the law and its functions "hazard a negative" because the implication of their claim was that if wrongs were righted and injustice eliminated, then the state and its laws would no longer be necessary. "To them," Savigny wrote, "the state appears as a necessary weapon of defence which might itself disappear or be dispensed with as superfluous under the presupposition of an extended or enlarged sense or feeling of right, or justice, or moral duty. Instead of that, the state, according to our view, would in that case, exhibit itself only the more noble and powerful."[14] The state, from this point of view, was not really responsible for supplying the content of justice but was responsible instead for ensuring that its content would be upheld. It was a surprisingly Kantian rendition of the relationship between the law and freedom. Reddie endorsed them both not only because the two characterisations of the law underpinned the difference between the law and morality but also because both of the characterisations made by Savigny and Kant made it clear that there was no further form of human association lying beyond the state. There was, therefore, no reason or need to expect the law to be replaced by morality itself or even, as Savigny had written, to reinforce the law by providing moral instruction. Instead, the law existed to provide the background conditions in which justice could coexist with expediency.

The dual quality of Smith's theory of justice, with its emphasis on both sides of the Ciceronian categories of the *honestum* and the *utile*, was part of a much larger family of late eighteenth-century discussions of the relationship between justice and utility, legality and morality, or duty and virtue. One side of this binary divide was compulsory, while the other was discretionary. The real Adam Smith Problem was not so much whether one side of the divide was selfish while the other was altruistic, but whether there was some mechanism that could ensure that both sides of the divide would work together without interfering with or undermining their respective purposes and capacities. The same problem, it is worth noting, also applied to the thought of both Jean-Jacques Rousseau and Immanuel Kant. For Rousseau the problem began with his distinction between the general will, which applied to all, and the will of all, which applied to the many smaller groups and partial associations to be found in any relatively complicated society. Recognising the difference, and subordinating the particularity of individual wills to the generality of the general will, called for a measure of self-abnegation, and this, Rousseau emphasised in his *Social Contract*, was the reason why every political society called for a measure of virtue, even though the political society in question was not a republic and did not have to rely on the type of underlying principle of virtue that Montesquieu had associated with both aristocratic and democratic forms of republican government. "That," Rousseau wrote in book 3, chapter 4 of his book, after listing all the requirements that a democracy would have to meet to be viable, "is why a famous author named virtue as the principle of a republic. For all these conditions could not exist without virtue. But, because he failed to make the necessary distinctions, this noble genius did not see that since the sovereign authority is everywhere the same, the same principle ought to apply to every well-constituted state, albeit to a greater or lesser degree according to the forming of government."[15]

Rousseau's invocation of virtue pointed, however, towards two different outcomes. In one guise, virtue could mean freedom of choice and an ability to subordinate present inclinations and preferences to a future or higher purpose. In this guise, virtue implied Kant's concept of autonomy and the freedom to choose one's own goals. In another guise, however, virtue could mean patriotic public service and a willingness to subordinate self-interest to the public interest. In this guise, virtue implied Robespierre's concept of republican morality and the primacy of the common good. But, if Rousseau's thought pointed prospectively towards either Kant or Robespierre, Kant's thought could also point retrospectively towards either Rousseau or Robespierre. Here, the problem was to identify a mechanism that could maintain the stability and durability of the distinction that Kant made between public law and private law. To Kant, public law had no content of its own because its content was supplied largely by private law. Public law on Kant's terms existed to maintain the legality and legitimacy of private law. At most, therefore, its content was more like a constitutional provision than any more substantive legislation. Again, however, it was not clear how to prevent the respective provisions of the public law–private law divide from overriding or undermining each other. In the light of these problems, what Oncken called the Adam Smith Problem was more generic than specific. Although, as his readers from Millar to Stewart and from Mackintosh to Reddie were careful to emphasise, Smith's system was designed to be compatible with justice as well as expediency, or with the honourable as well as the useful, it was not clear how it was possible to maintain a stable balance between the market and the state because it was not clear how to identify the means to articulate and keep together the moral and material dimensions of the two parts of a single economic and political system.

IX

Georg Wilhelm Friedrich Hegel—Civil Society and the State

IT WAS THE GERMAN PHILOSOPHER Georg Wilhelm Friedrich Hegel, with his version of the concept of civil society (*bürgerliche Gesellschaft*), who first conceived of a theoretical and practical bridge between the state and the market and, by extension, between justice and expediency. In narrow terms, Hegel's version of the concept of civil society was something like a synonym for the division of labour. As with the division of labour, it was made up of all those occupations and activities involved in the production, distribution, sale, and consumption of the many different agricultural and manufactured commodities available in a commercial society. But there was also a significant difference between the idea of the division of labour and Hegel's concept of civil society. This difference was that Hegel's concept housed both the many different occupations and activities involved in the division of labour, and many of the different organisations and institutions involved in the system of government. Although the English translation of Hegel's term *bürgerliche Gesellschaft* is usually given as "civil society," the French translation, *société bourgeoise* (bourgeois society), captures the meaning of the term more clearly because it refers more fully to its urban, corporate, and estate- or guild-based institutional and occupational content. With Hegel, the concept of civil society came to include the worlds of municipal government and the professions as well as property, industry, and trade. It could therefore include the figure of the administrator, the *fonctionnaire* or *Beamte*, and, because it did, it could also contain a third term, the administration, as a theoretical and practical bridge between the market and the state.

It is easy to underestimate the significance of the concept of administration in either modern political societies or modern political thought.[1] Hegel, notoriously, called the administration a "universal estate." It was, he wrote in his *Philosophy of Right* of 1821, part of the state and the system of estates that it housed.

It was, however, a special type of estate because, unlike the various other estates, the administrative estate was funded by the state itself out of the tax revenue supplied by civil society. In this sense, the administration was part of both civil society and the state. Unlike the other components of civil society, however, its resources were supplied by something other than itself. While those involved in agriculture, industry, trade, or the professions relied on their own resources to be able to survive and prosper, the administration had no resources of its own. This in turn meant that the relationship between the state and its administration was based, in the last instance, on finance, and that credit was a key component of the relationship between the state and its administration because the state itself was obliged to fund the costs of its administrative system and to manage

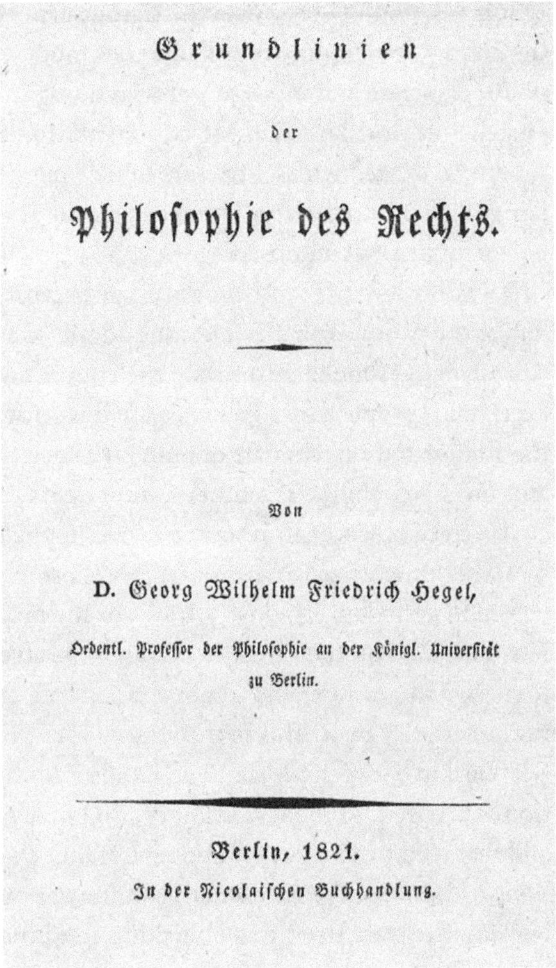

Grundlinien

der

Philosophie des Rechts.

Von

D. Georg Wilhelm Friedrich Hegel,

Ordentl. Professor der Philosophie an der Königl. Universität
zu Berlin.

Berlin, 1821.
In der Nicolaischen Buchhandlung.

FIGURE 6. Georg Wilhelm Friedrich Hegel, *Naturrecht und
Staatswissenschaft im Grundrisse* (1821)

the flows of income and expenditure running across its office-based bureaucracy.

Hegel was very familiar with the work of Adam Smith, but it is well known too that he was also fascinated by the thought of the eighteenth-century Scottish political economist Sir James Steuart and, in particular, by Steuart's unusually positive evaluation of public debt.[2] Hegel's treatment of the state bureaucracy or universal estate was, on the financial side, a development of the logic of Steuart's theory of public debt as a key component of a state. "The *universal estate*," Hegel explained, "has the *universal interests* of society as its business. It must therefore be exempted from work for the direct satisfaction of its needs, either by having private resources, or by receiving an indemnity from the state which calls upon its services, so that the private interest is satisfied by working for the universal."[3] This conflation of the private interest with the universal interest gave the administration its particular character. It was, Hegel added later, "integral to the definition of the *universal* estate—or more precisely, the estate which devotes itself to the service of the government—that the universal is the end of its essential activity."[4] It is important here to see what Hegel meant. What he did *not* mean was that the universal estate was an equivalent of Plato's guardians or China's mandarins. This was because Hegel's universal estate did not have to be equipped with a personal quality like knowledge, wisdom, or judgement, as was the case with a mandarin or guardian. It could, instead, rely on money, either to buy in services or to pay for the provision of public goods, and, equally importantly, could also rely on the law for providing a framework of rules to guide public and private life. Both, Hegel emphasised, had an intrinsically universal quality that obviated the need for any equivalent personal, or subjective, quality. "It is implicit in the organic unity of the powers of the state itself," he wrote, "that *one* and the same spirit decrees the universal and brings it to determinate actuality in implementing it."

It may at first seem remarkable that the state requires no direct services from the numerous skills, possessions, activities and talents [of its citizens] and from the infinitely varied living *resources* which these embody and which are at the same time associated with the disposition [of those who possess them], but lays claim only to the *one* resource which assumes the shape of *money*. . . . But money is not in fact one *particular* resource among others; on the contrary it is the universal aspect of all of them, in so far as they express themselves in an external existence in which they can be apprehended as *things*. Only at this extreme point of externality is it possible to determine services *quantitatively* and so in a just and equitable manner.[5]

The same quality belonged to the law, a subject that Hegel discussed alongside the subject of money in the same lemma. It was universal because it was rational, and this rationality meant, almost by definition, that a law was something less than a pure command (like "Thou shalt not kill"), but also something more than a purely factual description because it could also entail a permission or prohibition.[6] Its relationship to a state meant that the law was also more general than a command but was still less particular than a fact. Together, the combination of money and the law added up to both a fiscal state and a *Rechtsstaat*.

Civil society generated wealth, but civil society could also generate conflict. Conflict called for states, laws, and government. But states, laws, and government called for taxing and spending as well as regulating and ruling. Hegel's insight was to see that the position of the universal estate lying somewhere between the organisations and institutions of civil society and the organisations and institutions of the state meant that credit would be built into the evolving relationship between the regulating and ruling parts and the taxing and spending parts of the whole system. Since the universal estate had no resources of its own, leads and lags of income and expenditure would be entrenched within the whole administrative system, with the result that these credit-based leads and lags would mean that the state depended on civil society for its resources as strongly and deeply as civil society depended on the state for its security. The result, for the whole system, would be an embryonic capacity to measure, calculate, and project the allocation and distribution of resources within both civil society and the state and, because of the interrelationship of credit, interest rates, and the availability of capital, a further embryonic capacity for government to have a real economic policy. By identifying a third, administrative, term lying between the state and the market, Hegel began to identify the real dimensions of what was involved in creating a framework for thinking about politics in commercial society. Administration could be combined with public accountancy and public accountability, but it also gave rise to the problematic subject of administrative law, which was neither quite private nor quite public and, because of this, supplied many opportunities for the development of something analogous to the English Common Law with its emphasis on cases, precedents, and judicial interpretation.

The framework that Hegel began to establish also relied on two of the more obvious features of the division of labour, namely, its specialisation and differentiation. These features of the division of labour could be transferred readily to the idea of the separation of powers because specialisation and differentiation could be built as easily and cumulatively into an administration as into many other types of commercial, financial, or industrial organisation. On this basis, the old distinctions separating the legislative, executive, and judicial powers could be reinforced or modified by a potentially endless array of variations on the many different components of function, timing, content, or accountability built into all three powers. In itself, the old idea of the separation of powers was largely vertical with, at least analytically, clear lines of division separating the legislative, executive, and judicial powers. With the addition of Hegel's concept of an administration, the separation of powers could also be horizontal, with different powers exercised variously at, for example, municipal, district, regional, provincial, national, or federal levels. Finally, of course, the two types of separation of powers could be combined, with a vertical separation of powers applying as much at a municipal as at a federal level, but with some powers, like the power to print money or have a foreign policy, separated horizontally rather than vertically. The resulting proliferation of specialised administrative units and agencies would then have the further effect of broadening and deepening the interlocking system of leads and lags binding the state to civil society. On Hegel's terms, public debt and public administration were two sides of the same coin.

The fiscal and financial sides of the type of administrative system that, on Hegel's terms, could straddle the boundary separating civil society from the state had the further effect of creating an environment that was genuinely compatible with party politics. Usually, the growth of party politics has been taken to involve the adoption of procedures and practices that were first established in Britain in the seventeenth and eighteenth centuries because they were generated by the overlapping distinctions between Whigs and Tories, court and country, or government and opposition. But party politics existed in many other eighteenth-century European states, from the Swedish Hats and the Caps, to the various *négatifs*, *natifs*, and *représentants* of eighteenth-century Geneva and the Orangists and anti-Orangists of the United Provinces of the Netherlands. Clearly, all these versions of party politics called for the existence of what in the eighteenth century was often called a free state, usually because it housed a mixed or balanced system of government, with some measure of elected representation, religious latitude, a broadly free press, and a functioning legal system. But it also called for something more.

That addition was supplied by Hegel's three-sided distinction partitioning civil society, the state, and the administrative system. Together, the three parts of Hegel's system help to explain why British party politics could have turned into a more durable and stable party system earlier and more continuously than this transformation occurred in other European states. The addition of an administrative dimension helped, in the first place, to underline the importance of superimposing a fiscal and financial framework upon the relationship between local politics and national politics. The framework meant that the politics of the distribution and redistribution of individual and collective resources had a real public presence. It also, in the second place, highlighted the way that the many administrative units and electoral constituencies built into the interrelationship of civil society, the administration, and the state enabled parties and policies to be tried and tested in several different public settings before a decisive election occurred. This meant that the politics of public opinion could have the same public presence as the politics of distribution. Over the years, the politics of distribution and the politics of public opinion have become the driving force of electoral politics. The combination of administration, taxation, and public debt that Hegel identified helps to explain why it did.

Hegel's three-sided distinction of civil society, the state, and the administration was a development of a number of earlier examinations of political society and the division of labour made in the second half of the eighteenth century by Montesquieu, Rousseau, and Sieyès. The thought of the three individuals involved a substantial measure of continuity, which ensured that the content of their respective publications amounted to a real conceptual sequence. The sequence began with Montesquieu's concept of monarchy as a system of government in which, as he put it, one person ruled in conjunction with a number of subordinate, dependent, and intermediate powers, of which, he added, the most natural was a nobility. The most unusual feature of this combination of a royal sovereign and a number of subordinate, dependent, and intermediate powers was the division that it housed between a commercial and a noncommercial sector. The members of the nobility could own large amounts of property but were not allowed to trade. This meant that they would have to rely on intermediaries either to sell the products of their estates or to supply them with the goods that they needed both for future cycles of agricultural production and for their own consumption. Credit would, therefore, be built into the relationship between the commercial and noncommercial sectors, and, as Montesquieu explained, this would have a deep-seated effect on both the division of labour and the structure and composition of domestic and foreign trade. It meant that the French economy could be internationally competitive but would not have to compete solely, or even mainly, on price.

This competitive capacity applied as much to agriculture as it did to industry because its basis was a combination of product differentiation and technical innovation. Both, Montesquieu showed, were the effects of the relatively high levels of interest rates generated by the demand for credit produced by the initial division of the economy into commercial and noncommercial sectors. High levels of interest rates called for higher levels of profits, which in turn could be secured through a reliance either on market segmentation or on product cycles or intermittent combinations of the two. Market segmentation could involve specialisation in certain products or selling to certain regions or favouring certain customers or, again, intermittent combinations of them all. Product cycles could be generated by small changes in design, materials, or processes and the opportunities that they presented to producers to charge high prices at the start of the cycle and low prices at the end of the cycle by dumping surplus stock to raise cash flow. In this type of economy, cognac,

Camembert, champagne, or calvados mattered as much as *articles de Paris*, Lyonnais silks, or even denims from Nîmes. Montesquieu outlined its culture and structure carefully but epigrammatically and even went so far as to explain why the existence of some sixty thousand venal offices also favoured its stability and prosperity. Money made in trade could, two generations later, be translated into the status of nobility simply by means of acquiring an office. Here too the division between commercial and noncommercial sectors had a beneficial effect. It made the French nobility unusually open and, at the same time, relatively independent of centralised royal patronage and power. It also made it possible to see how trade, industry, and the division of labour could be combined with property, nobility, and authority. In the light of Montesquieu's concept of monarchy, the state could coexist with the market because, while both were clearly separate from one another, they were also clearly connected in a fundamentally symbiotic way. As was literally the case with symbiosis, they would live and die together.

Rousseau's approach to the subject of markets and the state was both more like and more unlike

Montesquieu's than is often assumed. As has been indicated, he rejected Montesquieu's assertion that only a republic needed to have virtue as its underlying motivating principle because, he maintained, sovereign power was a fundamental attribute of every political society and could, consequently, be used or abused under a broader range of conditions than those associated solely with democracies or aristocracies. But he also followed Montesquieu's concept of a two-sector society, with a commercial and a noncommercial sector that were distinct from one another but were still joined sufficiently tightly to require jointly what was needed for their common survival. In Rousseau's case, however, the difference between the two sectors was not supplied by a distinction between the nobility and the rest of society but was instead an effect of the elaborate system of election that, he argued, was required to produce the type of government that he called an "elected aristocracy." Rousseau called this electoral system a system of graduated or gradated promotion. In place of a noncommercial nobility and a commercial society, the idea of gradated promotion relied on election rather than inheritance to generate something like the same type of dual system to be found in Montesquieu's concept of monarchy. In this case, as was really the case in Rousseau's native city of Geneva, the two sides of the system were formed by trade and industry on the one side and by election and administration on the other. The idea underlying this variation on Montesquieu's system was that of an electorally generated filtering system, with every citizen electing the membership of the lowest level of political representation, such as a municipality or district, and with the members of these elected units then forming further levels of electors and elected to produce an elected aristocracy whose membership had climbed up the institutional hierarchy over several rounds of election and after a prolonged period of public scrutiny.

Rousseau described the system most fully in his *Considerations on the Government of Poland*, which was published for the first time in 1781 three years after his death. As several of his early readers noticed, there was a substantial measure of continuity between the plan that he set out there and those that began to be published by Condorcet and Pierre Samuel Dupont de Nemours in the decade after Rousseau's death. Both were closely associated with the reform agenda of the French

controller general of finances Anne Robert
Jacques Turgot during his brief period in office
from 1774 to 1776, and both also indicated the
similarities between Rousseau's idea of gradated
promotion and Turgot's plan to replace the old
French system of estate-based representation by a
system of local, regional, and national representation that, like Rousseau's, was designed to produce
a noncommercial political and administrative sector from a fully functioning commercial society.
This was the system that came to be called the
"representative system" by its most famous advocate, Emmanuel-Joseph Sieyès.

"All the work undertaken in society," Sieyès
wrote, "is representative."[7] As with Montesquieu
and Rousseau, this entailed a dual system. Sieyès's
own variation on this idea entailed the creation of
a pyramid-shaped system of political representation, with a democratic base, a monarchical or
presidential apex, and three intermediate levels of
political representation lying between them. Political representation would work by way of the
system of gradated promotion, where eligibility
for election to a higher office would depend on
one's having successfully discharged the duties of
a lower office. Everyone, however rich or well-
connected they might be, would have to start at

the bottom and work their way, step-by-step, up to the top. The system would also produce a nonpolitical, meritocratic elite that, like Montesquieu's idea of a nobility, would not be involved in trade but, unlike Montesquieu's nobility, would not be hereditary. The whole system would amount to what Sieyès called a *ré-publique* (or what we might call a modern, representative republic), as against either a *ré-privé* (absolute government) or a *ré-total* (Jacobin republicanism).

Sieyès repeatedly referred to the years around 1770 as the time when he began to formulate his system. "Work (*travail*) favours liberty only in becoming representative," he wrote in an undated note.

What seems to have been most applauded in France in Smith's work [the *Wealth of Nations*] is its first chapter on *the division of labour*. Yet there is nothing in his ideas that was not common among all those of my fellow citizens who took an interest in economic matters. . . . As for myself, I had gone further than Smith as from 1770. I saw not only that the *division* of labour in the same trade, namely, under *the same higher level of management*, was the surest way to reduce the costs and increase the quantity of

products, I also envisaged the *distribution* of
the great occupations or trades as the true
principle of the social state. . . . Multiply the
means, or the power, to satisfy our *needs*; enjoy
more, but work less (*jouir plus, travailler
moins*), this is what defines the natural increase
of liberty in the social state. Thus, the progress
of liberty follows naturally from the establishment of *representative* work.[8]

He made the point in print in the pamphlet entitled *Views of the Executive Means Available to the
Representatives of the Third Estate* that he published in the autumn of 1788. "The more a society
progresses in the arts of trade and production," he
wrote there, "the more apparent it becomes that
the work connected to public functions should,
like private employments, be carried out less ex-
pensively and more efficiently by men who make
it their exclusive occupation. This truth is well
known."[9] Later, in a note probably written in 1815,
he again referred back to the period around 1770
as the time when the idea had taken shape. Here,
the remark addressed not so much the representative character of the division of labour itself as
the related idea that *all* labour could be taken to

be productive, which was why, he wrote, the word *onéologie* was actually a more comprehensive, but far too obscure, name for political economy. The neologism, derived from the Greek words *oneō* and *logos*, was deliberately ambiguous and could mean both the science of profiting, acquiring, or benefiting and that of gratifying, delighting, or enjoying. To Sieyès, it was a word that filled a real theoretical and conceptual gap.

Properly speaking wealth consists of all existing values, but up to the present *onéologie* deals only with venal, or vendible, values. Ease, well-being, or, in a word, enjoyment (*jouissance*) are connected to many more goods than those that can be bought and sold, as well as to the large number of those that can be consumed without having been bought or sold at all. This observation alone serves to show that *onéologie* ought to cover a range that has yet to be noticed. Labour that anyone applies directly, as well as individual, collective, or public enjoyments (*jouissances*), indicate the immensity of the field of those elements of happiness that have yet to become the object of study. A good social state would combine things in such a way that those moral and physical enjoyments which are not bought or sold would still amount to a very considerable portion of each individual's well-being. Human industry and action seem to me to be very restricted if they are to be considered solely in terms of their vendible, or venal, products (see the *Analytical table of the universality of human enjoyment* that I made over forty years ago). The spectacle of a human society, considered in terms of general well-being, looks to me like a very poor thing if the individuals composing it are taken to be no more than a multitude of agents or instruments of vendible production, as if a political association has to be seen as no more than the formation of a great manufactory in which three classes of individuals— idle rentiers, active entrepreneurs, and laborious instruments—wage a silent war over how much of a share of the vendible product they will have. Production and consumption are correlates, even though they are rarely equal. Wealth which is destined to be sold, and even that part which could be sold even if it is not, amount to no more than the smallest proportion of consumption and production within the more general movement. *Onéologie* has not therefore been given all the extension that it should have as a *political science*. I spent some time on this point of view and made much progress in 1774 and the following years. It guided me in the project for establishing public festivals that I gave to the Committee on Public Education in 1793 etc. *Fata negarunt* (Fate ruled otherwise).[10]

Almost everything involved in human well-being could be incorporated into this comprehensively enlarged notion of political economy and, in addition, could be connected to the equally comprehensive idea of the division of labour as a representative system. If industry was the underlying principle of representation, then the range of activities to which the slogan *jouir plus, travailler moins* could be applied was virtually limitless. It is likely that this was the broad idea underlying the "Treatise on socialism" (*Traité du socialisme*) or, more elaborately, a "Treatise on socialism, or on the *goal* given by man to himself in society and of the *means* he has to attain it" (*Traité du socialisme, ou du but que se propose l'homme en société et des moyens qu'il a d'y parvenir*) that Sieyès envisaged but seems never to have written.[11]

Hegel's transformation of the idea of the division of labour into the concept of civil society, together with his description of the agonistic but complementary relationship between civil society and the state, had, in short, a largely French conceptual background. Montesquieu made the initial conceptual move with his description of a modern monarchy as a two-sector political system. Rousseau established the electoral character of a similarly divided two-sector system, while Sieyès associated both parts of his version of a two-sector system with the idea of the division of labour. The overlap between Sieyès and Hegel was substantial, but Hegel's move was to identify the administration as the conceptual and practical keystone of the whole edifice. One part of the administration was tied to civil society, but the other was tied to the state. Hegel gave the concept of administration a fuller and clearer status than it had been given by Montesquieu, Rousseau, and Sieyès. It was both a bridge and a buffer between civil society and the state. And, because it was both, it also had to rely on resources generated by both. Civil society could generate tax revenue, but the state could generate money. As David Ricardo went on to show, this was the combination that lay behind his concept of comparative advantage, the concept that still plays a part in theories of international trade. The basis of the concept was the idea that domestic monetary and financial policy could be used to enable, encourage, or even force different types of economic endowments and resources to grow and develop in reciprocally advantageous ways. Trade, from this perspective, did not have to be a zero-sum game and could, instead, turn into one in which everyone was a winner. Later, something like the same idea was transferred from the theory of international trade to the sphere of domestic politics. Here too, as Lorenz von Stein went on to show, the creation of currency involved in the growth of public debt had the effect of turning borrowing and lending into taxing and spending. On Stein's terms, only a state had the resources to keep the division of labour at bay. Stein called the outcome "social democracy." It was the domestic equivalent of Ricardo's concept of comparative advantage.

X

David Ricardo— Public Debt and Comparative Advantage

THE CONCEPT OF comparative advantage has come to be seen as one of the two great conceptual innovations of David Ricardo's *On the Principles of Political Economy* when it was published 1817.

The other was his corn model with its enduringly clear explanation of the interrelationship of the marginal productivity of land, the profits of agriculture, and the level of rent (a third concept, usually known as Ricardian equivalence, and meaning the equivalent cost of funding expenditure either from taxation or from debt, is also rel-

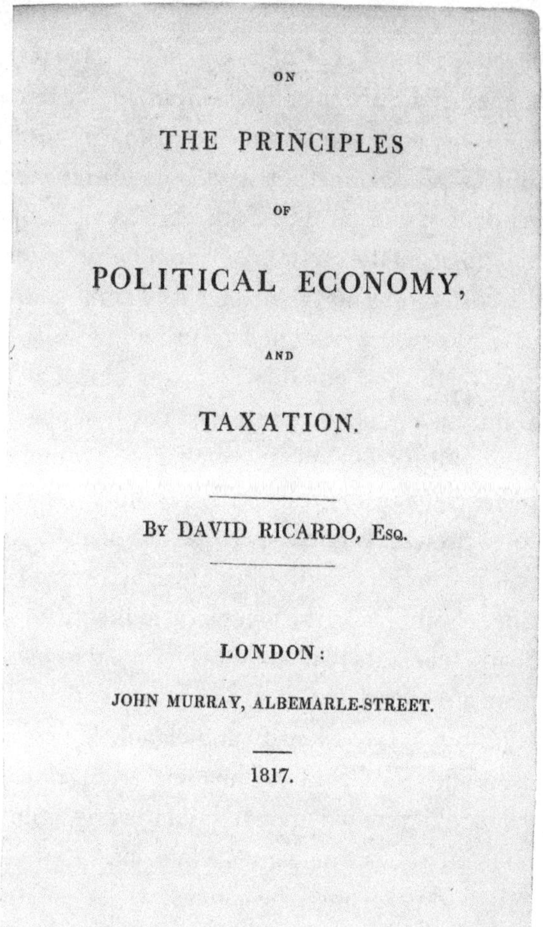

ON

THE PRINCIPLES

OF

POLITICAL ECONOMY,

AND

TAXATION.

By DAVID RICARDO, Esq.

LONDON:

JOHN MURRAY, ALBEMARLE-STREET.

1817.

FIGURE 7. David Ricardo, *On the Principles of Political Economy and Taxation* (1817)

evant). Although the two subjects were distinct because the concept of comparative advantage applied in the first instance to international trade, while the corn model applied primarily to the subject of taxation, they were not entirely independent of one another. Both were connected to the subject of the division of labour because both the corn model and the concept of comparative advantage were designed to provide guidance towards the best possible allocation of resources to produce the largest and least costly supply of commodities for as many members of a commercial society as possible. In this respect, the two concepts were variations on the idea of utility, or, as Adam Smith's followers put it, expediency. The aim of both was, in the first place, to identify a set of arrangements that could be designed to maximise individual and common utility and, in the second place, to identify and establish a corresponding set of fiscal and financial arrangements that could be relied upon to hold the first, utility-oriented, set of arrangements in place.

Ricardo explained the concept of comparative advantage in abidingly simple terms.[1] If a country like Britain produced cloth but did not produce wine, it had an obvious incentive to produce a lot more cloth than was needed for domestic consumption because the revenue produced by exporting the surplus could then be used to cover the costs of importing wine. But even if a country like Portugal produced both wine and cloth, it still had an advantage in specialising in wine, not cloth, because wine could be made more cheaply in Portugal while cloth could be produced more cheaply in Britain. If each country favoured its most productive economic sector, each country would have a larger surplus of the commodity that it produced available for export and, consequently, a greater capacity to import larger quantities of the commodity that it did *not* produce from the country that produced it more efficiently. Comparative advantage meant, in short, that everyone would be a winner.

Over the years, the concept of comparative advantage has come to be seen as a double-edged sword. On Ricardo's terms, it was designed to favour open markets, free trade, and frictionless transactions so that comparative advantage would work in ways that enabled poor underdeveloped economies to benefit as much as rich developed economies. To its critics, both in Ricardo's time and now, comparative advantage has usually been said to have had the opposite effect. Instead of reciprocity it has produced dependence; instead of rebalancing the relationship between rich countries and poor countries, it has magnified their inequality; instead of a way out of the world of empire, slavery, and exploitation, it has generated the development of underdevelopment and favoured the formation of a modern world system divided comprehensively between a capitalist West and an exploited rest.[2] On this interpretation, the solution to the problems built into the concept of comparative advantage has come to resemble Louis Blanc's solution to the problems built into what, then, was his novel concept of capitalism. Capitalism, for Blanc, was the product of the private ownership of capital. Its beneficiaries were its owners, while its victims were those without capital. The solution was the nationalisation, or socialisation, of capital and the substitution of endogenous development (or development from within) for the real underdevelopment that had been exogenously imposed (or imposed from without).

Here too, however, the initial problem was not capitalism but the division of labour. Ricardo could see this very clearly both because it was something that Jean-Jacques Rousseau had described two generations earlier and because it had been amplified and discussed by his close friend Thomas Robert Malthus in his famous *Essay on the Principle of Population* of 1798 and, subsequently, in the long and animated private correspondence that Ricardo conducted not only with Malthus, but also with his other political economist friends, Sismondi, Mackintosh, and Jean-Baptiste Say. As Rousseau had pointed out, the fundamental problem with the division of labour was that it superimposed a spurious uniformity on different types of commodities and the needs that they were supposed to meet. Cloth was certainly exchangeable for wine, but individual consumers are usually more likely to buy a glass of wine a day than a piece of cloth a day. The same absence of comparability was even more strongly pronounced in the difference between subsistence goods like wheat, rye, or bread and items of discretionary consumption like portable phones, television sets, or microwave ovens. People have to eat and drink in order to survive, but they do not need to phone or watch TV to survive.

Rousseau's initial point, therefore, was that the idea of comparative advantage seemed to reach its limits when it ran into human survival needs. Since everyone has to eat and drink, everyone needs a supply of basic subsistence goods; if this is the case, subsistence goods will frequently be produced under highly suboptimal conditions, and this, in turn, will mean that the costs of producing to meet survival needs will be relatively high, while the returns to the producers will be commensurately low. This, as Rousseau emphasised, meant that the producers of goods that were most fundamental for human survival were very much more likely to be poorly rewarded than those who produced things covered by discretionary expenditure. Agricultural production, he claimed, usually went hand in hand with poverty, but making jewellery did not. In this light, the development of the division of labour coupled with the concept of comparative advantage seemed to lead, at best, to a dead end and, at worst, to a far more literal version of human fatality.

Interestingly, and particularly in the light of his bleak diagnosis, Rousseau did not give up on the division of labour. Nor, though perhaps less surprisingly, did Ricardo. This is because the related concepts of comparative advantage and the division of labour can be described in two different ways. One way is to focus on commodities and the needs that they could meet. Another way, however, is to focus on the same set of commodities but this time to highlight the value that they could have. Since, as Rousseau had emphasised, these needs and values have very little relationship to each other, the differences between needs and values displayed by almost every type of commodity could be used to make the idea of comparative advantage work under conditions of real human diversity rather than under the conditions of the spurious uniformity imposed by markets and prices. This was Ricardo's real insight and, contrary to the later caricatures produced by his Marxist critics, the key to his version of the concept of comparative advantage.

The full title of Ricardo's most famous book was *The Principles of Political Economy and Taxation*. This, at least in part, was because the concept of comparative advantage had as much to do with taxation as it had to do with trade. The subject that encompassed both trade and taxation was, however, the subject of money and its relationship to both a national bank and a national debt. Ricardo spent some time thinking and writing about all three of these subjects. He incorporated part of a pamphlet entitled *Proposals for an Economical and Secure Currency* that he published in 1816 into chapter 27, dealing with currency and banks, of his *Principles of Political Economy* and, at the time of his death, was still at work on a second pamphlet entitled *Plan for the Establishment of a National Bank* that was published posthumously in 1824. A strong case could be made to argue that the subjects of money, banking, and debt were the keys to Ricardo's treatment of trade and comparative advantage because, as he set out to show, they provided much of the leverage that was to be used to turn the differences between needs and values into the foundation of a system of trade based on comparative advantage. Ricardo's interest in money and debt was long-standing, partly because he was a banker and partly because of the public prominence acquired by the two subjects during the period of the French revolutionary and Napoleonic wars. The starting point was the decision taken in 1797 by William Pitt's government to fund the costs of war by issuing a paper currency that, among other things, could be used by the Bank of England, without gold or silver security, to purchase government debt. The decision, taken more or less concurrently with the almost total collapse of the French paper currency, the *assignat*, between 1793 and 1799, gave rise to a protracted public debate during the following dozen years over what came to be called "the currency principle" and "the bullion principle." At issue was the extent to which the levels of prices, production, and prosperity were determined either by the quantity of money in circulation or by a specified ratio between the currency and gold or silver bullion and its putatively positive effects on price stability, production, and productivity.

Ricardo's position was that a well-designed financial and fiscal system would make it possible to have the benefits of both the currency principle and the bullion principle. This in turn would make it possible to reconcile the real benefits of comparative advantage with the real differences in human needs and circumstances. In this respect, his argument for a fiscally and financially based currency was rather like Hegel's argument in favour of a state-funded system of administration. The fundamental attribute of the two systems was credit. For Hegel, credit was built into the hierarchy of administrative institutions that straddled civil society and the state. The absence of any independent source of income in the administration meant that it would have to rely as much on borrowing and lending as on taxing and spending. The same applied to Ricardo's idea of a paper currency. It too would be credit based, and, because it was, its value and stability would have to be tied to a fiscal and financial reserve. "A currency," he wrote, "is in its most perfect state when it consists wholly of paper money, but of paper money of an equal value with the gold which it professes to represent. The use of paper instead of gold, substitutes the cheapest in place of the most expensive medium, and enables the country, without loss to any individual, to exchange all the gold which it before used for this purpose, for raw materials, utensils and food; by the use of which, both its wealth and its enjoyments are increased."[3]

Ricardo made it clear that the quantity of a paper currency that could be issued would have to be limited by subjecting the institution responsible for its creation, whether it was the state or an institution like the Bank of England, to the obligation to pay its notes either in gold coin or in bullion. In addition, there could be a set of commissioners, or something like a National Bank or a Federal Reserve, with the power to issue the paper currency "totally independent of the control of ministers," as Ricardo put it.[4] This fiat currency would be something like the long-established national debt, but it would not bear interest. The commissioners could, therefore, use it to manage the rate of interest on the real national debt by purchasing quantities of debt and issuing equivalent quantities of the currency to do so. This, in conjunction with the reserve requirements that would set a ceiling on the quantity of paper currency to be issued, would enable the commissioners to manage interest rates in ways that could be combined with the more directly political and accountable process of managing taxation to bring the relationship between needs and values into what, in the final analysis, was a more moral alignment. Taxes on goods with a high value but a low utility could be used to offset tax exemptions on goods with a low value and a high utility. Tax revenue could also be used to maintain gold reserves and, consequently, loosen the constraints on the money supply, while, in other circumstances, the opposite types of procedure could apply. Comparative advantage, in this setting, was a product of fiscal and financial incentives or disincentives as much as it was an effect of costs and productivity. It could accommodate changes of

policy as well as changes in the underlying economies of both rich states and poor states because
its real foundations were not to be found in the
relative costs of imported or exported commodities but in the financial and fiscal systems on
which both importers and exporters were obliged
to rely. With Ricardo, monetary policy and fiscal
policy could be used to manage markets, and, as
a result, capital could be used to neutralise, offset,
or circumvent the otherwise relentless logic of
the division of labour and the proliferating im-
peratives of the various types of commercial society that it brought in its wake. Empires existed
long before—and long after—the idea of comparative advantage. There is no reason to conflate
Ricardo's distinctive concept with the more generic concept of empire.

XI

Lorenz von Stein— Public Debt and Public Administration

RICARDO'S ARGUMENT applied in the first instance to foreign trade and to the relationship between rich countries and poor countries. The same type of argument, however, was also used to explain how capital could be made to neutralise, but not replace, the market in a domestic context and, by so doing, to address the divisions between the rich and the poor at home rather than abroad. This was the argument underlying the distinction between the constitution and the administration of a state that supplied much of the conceptual

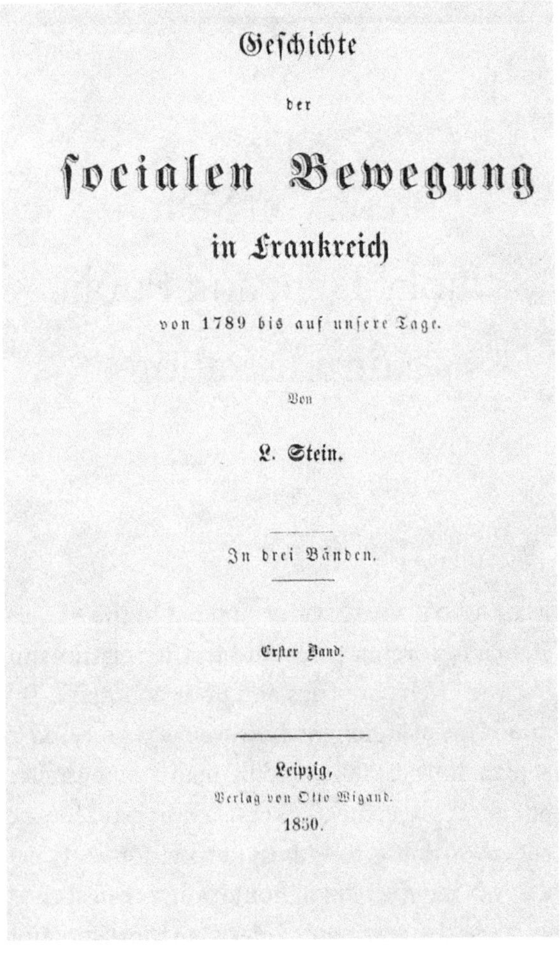

Geschichte

der

socialen Bewegung

in Frankreich

von 1789 bis auf unsere Tage.

Von

L. Stein.

In drei Bänden.

Erster Band.

Leipzig,
Verlag von Otto Wigand.
1850.

FIGURE 8. Lorenz von Stein, *Geschichte der socialen Bewegung in Frankreich von 1789 bis auf unsere Tag* (1850)

architecture of the *History of the Social Movement in France, 1789–1850*, published in 1850 by the Danish-German-Austrian legal theorist Lorenz von Stein.[1] As Stein presented it, the distinction added a further dualism to those that could already be found in the commercial-noncommercial, sovereignty-government, and public-private distinctions. It did so, he argued, because modern constitutional principles applied essentially to individuals, while modern administrative principles applied essentially to groups.

As with the other distinctions, the problem was to find a way to ensure that both sets of principles could be accommodated within a single state. Constitutional principles applied to individuals, regardless of their various circumstances, endowments, and life chances. Administrative principles applied to groups, precisely because of their various circumstances, endowments, and life chances. The first existed to secure formal equality, while the second existed to establish real social cohesion. As Stein recognised, combining the two sets of principles amounted to an embryonic theory of social democracy. "The transition from democracy towards this new configuration," he wrote, "is already apparent in the idea of social democracy.

At present, the content of that idea is still obscure and if it does not emerge from that obscurity, it will disappear. But if it does emerge, it will have to become a *theory of society*, and then *the future will belong to it*."[2]

The argument was made at the end of the great cycle of revolutions that swept across Europe in 1848 and relied very heavily on Hegel's state–civil society distinction. Stein's version of the nexus formed by the state, civil society, and the administration centred on money, credit, and public debt. He explained why it did most fully in the long introduction that he wrote to his *History of the Social Movement in France*. The title of that introduction—"The Concept of Society and Its Laws of Motion"—was, as Stein went on to argue, designed to indicate that the concept of the state had to be matched by a concept of society.[3] Putting the two together, Stein claimed, would become the basis of a theory of state action that would be both compatible with, but also distinct from, society.

The starting point of Stein's theory of state action was the problematic relationship between individual autonomy and social interdependence. As was the case with many earlier theorists of the division of labour from Rousseau to Hegel, the problem was generated by the initial tension between individual needs and desires, on the one hand, and the limited amount of time and ability that any individual had available to meet them. The obvious solution to this tension, Stein wrote, was the division of labour. But the development of the division of labour gave rise to a further array of problems about information, coordination, and rules. Something more than interpersonal reciprocity was needed to provide a common will to meet these common needs. This, Stein argued, was what a state could do. It was also why it made sense to define the state as simply "a community manifesting its actions and will through its personality."[4] Personality, according to Stein, was, therefore, the principle of the state. It was the name that could be given to the state's ability to unite and coordinate individual wills in ways that enabled them to realise everything that was best in each and every individual personality. The claim was redolent of the long-drawn-out German-language discussions of the reasons for the Creation and the purpose of human existence—discussions that, in the early nineteenth century, had given rise to the theological and anthropological speculations of

Friedrich Schleiermacher, Ludwig Feuerbach, and August Cieszkowski that played readily into Marx's philosophy of history. As in those earlier discussions, Stein's version of the answer had a clear moral and historical goal. Given, he wrote, that the state was made up of individuals, it followed that "the measure of development of every individual is the measure of development of the state itself."[5]

Stein's argument appeared, however, to lead towards two apparently incompatible conclusions. If, on the one hand, the state's development was predicated on every aspect of individual material, cultural, and spiritual development, it seemed to follow that its constitution had to make as much provision as possible for all of its members to be as fully involved as possible in the life of both the state and its government. From another point of view, however, the same emphasis on the symbiotic relationship between individual personality and the personality of the state seemed to mean that the state itself would be radically dependent on its members' resources and capacities. If the state was supposed to enable its members to become as fully themselves as possible, it seemed to be bereft of the means to do so.

Although, because it was simply the locus of the division of labour, civil society was subordinate to the state, the reality, in fact, was entirely the opposite. "The state," as Stein put it, "has no real existence outside of society."[6] But society was, by definition, an acquisitive society (a phrase that Stein was one of the first to use) because, in an important sense, it was predicated on the aspirations and ambitions of a multitude of increasingly differentiated individual personalities, while the identity of the state was predicated on the other hand on a single common personality. In a state, individual personality was combined with the unitary personality of the state, but in civil society individual personality was differentiated from every other individual personality. The combination of the drive for unity and the drive for individuality and individual acquisition meant that the state-society relationship was based on a radical contradiction. As Stein went on to show, this meant that while personality, or a single will made up of an integrated combination of unity and multiplicity, was the underlying principle of the state, the underlying principle of society was actually interest, or a centrifugal combination of diversity and difference generated by the division of labour.[7] The two principles were not only radically at odds with one another, but were also locked into a power relationship in which the state would, in effect, be little more than a target waiting to be captured by one or another of its predatory components.

The contradiction not only supplied a framework for explaining why, as Stein went on to describe it, the history of the social movement in France was a history of class struggle, but it also seemed to show, more generally, why any claim about the compatibility between individual personality and the personality of the state was condemned to end in a double bind.[8] If the personality of the state supplied the means to manage the division of labour, the division of labour was, inversely, the source of the individual drives and inequalities of property, capital, time, and money that ruled out the idea of a state personality. The dilemma soon gave rise to a number of putative solutions. One solution, usually associated with Marx and his followers, was to try to eliminate the state, while another, sometimes associated with Proudhon, was to try to dissolve the state into as many self-governing institutions as possible. Stein's solution was to remain closer to Hegel's concept of the state, but to combine it with a radically different theory of state power and state action.

Stein's theory of state power and state action was fiscal and financial in character. It was fiscal because a functioning fiscal system called for a comprehensive administrative system, made up not only of a body of tax officials, but also of further clusters of legal, financial, and property-related offices to supply the information and procedures required by the functional ramifications of the fiscal system itself. This meant that a bureaucratically organised administrative system, comparable to Hegel's own idea of a universal estate, would have to be the other side of what, as Stein also emphasised, would be a highly inclusive political constitution. While a constitution was the means by which individuals, with their individual personalities, could have a real relationship to the state, and to the personality of the state, an administrative system was the means to ensure that the two types of personality would be kept distinct.

As with Hegel, an administrative system was the keystone of a commercial society because it

was the one institution that actually existed on
both sides of the state–civil society divide. Without a constitution and with no proper administration, Stein argued, individuals would simply turn
towards monarchy as the most obvious embodi-
ment of the idea of the state.[9] Trying to maintain
a viable distinction between individuals and the
state under the aegis of a genuinely democratic
regime would be even more difficult because the
separation of the public from the private built
into a bureaucracy would dissolve into a reiter-
ated and more morally demanding game of role
switching. The concept of a democratic bureaucracy was a concept too far. On Stein's terms, representative government, from this point of view,
required a bureaucratic state.

Importantly, however, the core of Stein's theory
of state power and state action was more financial
than fiscal and relied as much on monetary as on
administrative or bureaucratic means. This, Stein
claimed, was because the one self-evident sign of
a sovereign state was its ability to create money
and, by extension, to manage and preserve a stable currency. This claim meant that public debt
was the real mechanism with the power to reconcile the state and civil society because the finan-

cial resources that the state could generate had
the potential to overcome the contradiction between multiple individual personalities and its
own single personality. The financial resources in
question could do so, Stein argued, because the
funds borrowed by the state could be added to
the pool of private capital both by means of a de-
centralised system of interest-free loans and,
more generally, because borrowing funds would
remove smaller amounts of capital from society
than taxation would, while payments of interest
on debt would ensure that some of the borrowed
funds would go back into circulation. The state-
backed flows of income and expenditure generated by public debt would be managed by the
bureaucracy, but the resources themselves would
be allocated by means of decisions within a con-
stitutionally specified institutional network.
Monetary and financial policy could be used,
therefore, to offset the divisions generated by private property to enable the propertyless to acquire the education, skills, and capital required
for economic survival in an acquisitive society.

"A state without a debt," Stein observed famously, "either cares too little for its future or de-
mands too much from its present."[10] Trade without

credit, he wrote elsewhere, was "like a bird without wings," while credit itself was rather like the clothes that parents would buy for their children: the right measure had to be several sizes too large.[11] Seen this way, Stein claimed, public debt went together with "social democracy." In his usage, there was a real significance to both parts of the phrase. The democratic side applied to the constitution and its arrangements, while the social side applied to the bureaucracy and its provisions. "The principle of social democracy," Stein concluded, "is therefore *universal suffrage* inasmuch as it has to do with the constitution and the *abolition of social dependence* in the working class and inasmuch as it has to do with the administration. In social democracy, the constitution is the democratic element, while the administration is the social element." The combination, he added, was the "natural and unavoidable outcome of the liberal movement."[12]

Capital, on Stein's terms, was the means to neutralise capitalism or, alternatively, to make capitalism safe for social democracy. In one sense, the idea was similar to Louis Blanc's because its starting point was an analogous distinction between capital and capitalism. But Stein's idea was also radically different from Louis Blanc's idea because it relied on money and markets rather than associations and cooperation as solutions to the related problems of inequality, injustice, and exploitation. Louis Blanc's solution was predicated on replacing private property by public property, including the public ownership of capital. Stein's solution was predicated on the recognition of monetary sovereignty as one of the main attributes of a state, and on the further recognition of financial and fiscal policy as two of the cornerstones of democratic politics. This is what they still seem to be.

XII

Conclusion

THE AIM OF THIS ESSAY has been to try to explain why the distinction between capitalism and commercial society is worth making. The concept of capitalism began as a term that was used to refer to the private ownership of capital. It was, in short, a property theory; and, because it was a property theory, it could refer as much to individuals and individual ownership as to collectivities and common ownership, including types of ownership that could be said to be negative as much as positive. The concept of a commercial society on the other hand presupposed something more than property and ownership, irrespective of whether the property in question was individual or collective and whether the type of ownership was negative or positive. It presupposed the division of labour. Unlike property, it is not usual, at least in the first instance, to associate the idea of the division of labour with individual activity because the idea of the division of labour calls, minimally, for more than one individual. Robinson Crusoe might well, as Marx pointed out, have been the prototype of proprietary capitalism and the foresight and ingenuity that came with it, but his island existence was a long way away from the division of labour.[1] The division of labour carried out by a single individual is usually called multitasking.

The concept of a commercial society was not, therefore, a property theory. It was instead, and as its name implies, a theory of society. As Smith and Marx both recognised, it was a theory of a society in which individuals are radically dependent upon one another because this, ultimately, is what the division of labour can do. In this respect, the watchwords of a commercial society can be found in the famous first lines of Jean-Jacques Rousseau's *Social Contract* of 1762. "Man," he wrote "is born free, but is everywhere in chains. Those who believe themselves to be masters of others are still greater slaves than those they rule. How did this change occur? I do not know. If I [were] to be asked, however, what can make it legitimate, I believe that I am able to answer this question."[2]

Rousseau's answer supplied many of the ideas and concepts discussed in this essay. It is conceivable that it also supplied Smith with the starting point of his never-to-be-completed discussion of how the subjects of justice and expediency—or justice and utility—could both be fundamental to a single political society. This is because the second part of Rousseau's description of how freedom had turned into slavery did not involve turning slavery back into freedom but simply asserted instead that it was possible to make the change legitimate. Quite a lot, in the light of this acknowledgement, hangs on the word "legitimate," and part of the point of this essay has been to provide a very schematic indication of the scale of the ground that has had to be covered to get within sight of what legitimacy can involve. As should be clear by now, the ground in question was not only a matter of government, states, and the law, or even, as Rousseau put it, an inquiry into the nature of the social contract, but was also made up as much of the law and legal policy, money and monetary policy, commerce and commercial policy as it was made up of the myriads of ordinary arrangements of civil society and the fiscal and financial institutions of the state. The positive side of this level of complexity is its complexity. So too, sadly, is its negative side.

Complexity, however, calls for thought and for trying to work out the many different things that complicated things actually entail. This is why it is worth finding out more about the early nineteenth-century interest in administration, money, and fiscal policy together with the types of social and political arrangements that could house them. Seen in context, these were the subjects that were once taken to form the basis of a now-forgotten set of answers to the problem of the division of labour. They did so not because any one of them could supply something ready-made but because, together, they were taken to be able to provide the concepts and the information that made thinking about politics and policy in a commercial society possible. In simple systems, if something goes wrong, everything can go wrong. In complicated systems, small changes in one part can either be restricted to that single part, or can have positive effects in other parts, or can be circumvented or neutralised by the addition of further parts. Capitalism, in older renditions, had a built-in capacity for catastrophe. Part of the point of this essay has been to suggest that the division of labour is worse. This is because capitalism, and not only in Marx's rendition, really does house the possibility of alternatives to capitalism. Even if the expropriators have not all been expropriated, and need and use have not really come back into their own, property and ownership, including the ownership of capital, really do change. It is less clear that there can be any equivalent change to the division of labour because all the many variations on the idea of collective multitasking—from decentralisation to federalisation to multiple organisational units to vertical and horizontal integration to flexible specialisation—look suspiciously like the division of labour in a different guise. The name may change, but the thing itself looks as if it is here to stay.

There have been many alternatives to capitalism, but, as both Ricardo and Hegel recognised, it is far from clear that there is any alternative to the division of labour, other than, simply, its absence. The archaic term "commercial society," with its now bleakly ambiguous eighteenth-century undertones of *doux commerce*, is, it seems, more firmly entrenched than its apparently more modern equivalent, capitalism. The many ramifications of the division of labour that commercial societies have come to house are, consequently, more intricate, deep-seated, and complicated than even the surprisingly capacious idea of property seems to have been able to accommodate. As Lorenz von Stein recognised, the concept of social democracy, with its connotations of political inclusiveness and social justice, refers as much to the idea of the division of labour as it does to the noun and the adjective contained in its name. In the nineteenth century, before the idea of a commercial society came to be largely swallowed up by the concept of capitalism, a great deal of careful, imaginative, and creative thought went into trying to work out what to do about both the positive and the negative sides of the division of labour. The question of how to reconcile the two sides gave rise to many, now largely forgotten, discussions of private international law, currency and customs unions, tariff and trade regimes, and, more broadly, of the origins and nature of the type of dual political system that was once associated with the thought of Jean-Jacques Rousseau and Adam Smith. It was not hard, in a world made up of sovereign states, to identify a gap between the local purchase of government policies and the global reach of the division of labour. It was also not hard, even in a world made up of sovereign states, to think about how to bridge that gap by examining the causal properties of the types of fiscal and financial policies, legal arrangements, and political institutions that were once taken to be compatible with the distinctions between markets and politics, expediency and justice, and civil society and the state that were once associated with the concept of a commercial society. Some of that thought, but only a very small part of it, has formed the subject matter of this book. Quite a lot more will be required for what could come next.

NOTES

Preface

1. The book in question was Richard Passow, *Kapitalismus, eine begrifflich-terminologische Studie* [1918] (Jena, Gustav Fischer, 1927). For the review, see Henri Hauser, "Kapitalismus," *Revue d'économie politique* 41 (1927): 1201–2. For a recent overview of many of the established views of the subject, see Geoff Mulgan, *The Locust and the Bee* [2013] (Princeton, NJ, Princeton UP, 2015).

2. Joseph Benoit, *Belgicismes ou les vices de langage et de prononciation les plus communs en Belgique corrigés d'après l'Académie et les meilleurs écrivains* (Antwerp, 1857), p. 12. For fuller discussion of the subject of words ending in "-ism," see the final chapter of Michael Sonenscher, *The Romans, the Germans and the Moderns: An Essay on the Foundations of Modern Politics* (Princeton, NJ, Princeton UP forthcoming).

3. "Ce sont des mots excessivement creux, mais qui servent de jalons au public." Jules Husson (aka Champfleury), *Contes d'automne* (Paris, 1854), p. 99.

4. Edmond Silberner, "Le mot capitalisme," *Annales d'histoire sociale* 2 (1940): 133–34. See too Jürgen Kocka, "Capitalism: The Re-emergence of a Historical Concept," *International Social History Association Newsletter* 5 (2016): 1–26 and the further

secondary literature cited there, together with Pierre Rosanvallon, *Notre histoire intellectuelle et politique 1968–2018* (Paris, Seuil, 2018), pp. 340–49.

5. "Criez donc: Vive le *capital*! Nous applaudirons et nous attaquerons avec autant plus de vivacité le *capitalisme*, son ennemi mortel. Vive la poule aux œufs d'or, et défendons-la contre qui l'éventre." Louis Blanc, *Organisation du travail* [1839], 9th ed. (1850), p. 162, cited by Silberner, "Le mot capitalisme," p. 133. Compare this passage to the entries on "Capitalisme" and "Travail" in Jean-Numa Ducange, Razmig Keucheyan, and Stéphanie Roza, eds., *Histoire globale des socialismes* (Paris, PUF, 2021), pp. 76–87, 609–20. On Louis Blanc, see chapter 5 below.

6. For a recent overview of both, see Andrew David Edwards, Peter Hill, and Juan Neves-Sarriegui, "Capitalism in Global History," *Past & Present* 249 (2020): e1–e32. See too Sebastian Conrad, *What Is Global History?* (Princeton, NJ, Princeton UP, 2016), and Bernd-Stefan Grewe and Karin Hofmeester, eds., *Luxury in Global Perspective: Objects and Practices, 1600–2000* (Cambridge, CUP, 2016). For two recent and absorbing contributions to capitalist studies, but with more limited discussion of the subjects of commercial society and the division of labour, see Charly Coleman, *The Spirit of French Capitalism: Economic Theology in the Age of Enlightenment* (Stanford, CA, Stanford UP, 2021), and William H. Sewell Jr., *Capitalism and the Emergence of Civic Equality in Eighteenth-Century France* (Chicago, U of Chicago Press, 2021).

Chapter I. Capitalism and Commercial Society

1. On the subject, see Daniel Luban, "Adam Smith on Vanity, Domination, and History," *Modern Intellectual History* 9 (2012): 275–302, and, more fully and directly, Istvan Hont, *Politics in Commercial Society: Adam Smith and Jean-Jacques Rousseau*

(Cambridge, MA, Harvard UP, 2015), plus, most recently, Paul Sagar, *Adam Smith Reconsidered: History, Liberty, and the Foundations of Modern Politics* (Princeton, NJ, Princeton UP, 2022).

2. For a recent example, see Maria Pia Paganelli, "Adam Smith and the Origins of Political Economy," *Social Philosophy and Policy* 37 (2020): 159–69.

3. Adam Smith, *An Inquiry into the Nature and Causes of the Wealth of Nations* [1776], 2 vols., ed. R. H. Campbell, A. S. Skinner, and W. B. Todd (Oxford, OUP, 1976), bk. 1, ch. 4, p. 37. On the phrase and the concept of the division of labour, see the editorial note on pp. 12–13 of the same edition.

4. Ibid., bk. 1, ch. 3, p. 31.

5. Ibid., vol. 2, bk. 5, ch. 1, sec. f, p. 784.

6. For examples of these approaches, see Silvia Federici, *Caliban and the Witch: Women, the Body and Primitive Accumulation* (New York, Autonomedia, 2004); Marcel van der Linden and Karl Heinz Roth, eds., *Beyond Marx: Theorizing the Global Labour Relations of the Twenty-First Century* (Leiden, Brill, 2014); Jason Moore, *Capitalism in the Web of Life: Ecology and the Accumulation of Capital* (London, Verso, 2015); Immanuel Wallerstein, *The Modern World System*, 3 vols. (New York, Academic Press, 1974–89); Fernand Braudel, *Capitalism and Civilization*, 3 vols. (London, Collins, 1982–85); Immanuel Wallerstein, ed., *The Modern World-System in the* Longue Durée [2004] (Oxford, Routledge, 2016); Giovanni Arrighi, *The Long Twentieth Century: Money, Power and the Origins of Our Times* (London, Verso, 1994) and his earlier "Capitalism and the Modern World System," *Review* (Fernand Braudel Center) 21 (1998): 113–29; Bruce R. Scott, *The Concept of Capitalism* (New York, Springer, 2009). For a wide-ranging collection of essays, see Maxine Berg, ed., *Writing the History of the Global* (Oxford, OUP, 2013) and, more recently, her review essay "Commodity Frontiers: Concepts and History," *Journal of Global*

History 16 (2021): 1–5, doi:10.1017/S1740022821000036. See also Vanessa Ogle, "Time, Temporality and the History of Capitalism," *Past & Present* 243 (2019): 312–27, and her earlier "Whose Time Is It? The Pluralization of Time and the Global Condition, 1870s–1940s," *American Historical Review* 118 (2013): 1376–1402; Pierre Dockès, *Le capitalisme et ses rythmes*, 2 vols. (Paris, Classiques Garnier, 2019–21), and compare Onur Ulas Ince, *Colonial Capitalism and the Dilemmas of Liberalism* (Oxford, OUP, 2018), to John Shovlin, *Trading with the Enemy: Britain, France and the 18th Century Quest for a Peaceful World Order* (New Haven, CT, Yale UP, 2021).

7. Adam Smith, *Lectures on Jurisprudence* [1762–63], ed. R. L. Meek, D. D. Raphael, and P. G. Stein (Oxford, OUP, 1978), p. 352. See also p. 493: "Thus we have shewn that different genius is not the foundation of this disposition to barter, which is the cause of the division of labour. The real foundation of it is that principle to perswade which so much prevails in human nature." On these passages, see Andreas Kalyvas and Ira Katznelson, "The Rhetoric of the Market: Adam Smith on Recognition, Speech and Exchange," *Review of Politics* 63 (2001): 549–79; Warren J. Samuels and W. Henderson, "The Etiology of Adam Smith's Division of Labor: Alternative Accounts and Smith's Methodology Applied to Them," in *Essays in the History of Economics*, ed. Warren J. Samuels et al. (New York, Routledge, 2004), pp. 8–89; and Warren J. Samuels, "Adam Smith's 'History of Astronomy' Argument: How Broadly Does It Apply? And Where Do Propositions Which 'Sooth the Imagination' Come From?," *History of Economic Ideas* 15 (2007): 53–78.

8. "Property, which at first was limited to the animals that a man killed, his weapons, his nets, and his cooking utensils, later came to include his cattle and eventually was extended to the earth that he won from its virgin state and cultivated. On the death of

the owner this property naturally passed into the hands of his family, and in consequence some people came to possess a surplus that they could keep. If this surplus was absolute, it gave rise to new needs, but if it existed only in one commodity and at the same time there was a scarcity of another, this state of affairs naturally suggested the idea of exchange, and from then onwards, moral relations grew in number and increased in complexity." Marie-Jean-Antoine-Nicolas, marquis de Condorcet, *Sketch for a Historical Picture of the Progress of the Human Mind* [1793], in *Condorcet: Selected Writings*, ed. Keith Michael Baker (Indianapolis, IN, Bobbs Merrill, 1976), p. 212. For the French, see Condorcet, *Tableau historique des progrès de l'esprit humain: Projets, Esquisse, Fragments et Notes (1772–1794)*, ed. Jean-Pierre Schandeler and Pierre Crépel (Paris, INED, 2004), p. 236: "Cette propriété se transmet à la famille à la mort de son chef. Quelques uns possèdent un superflu susceptible d'être conservé. S'il est absolu, il fait naître de nouveaux besoins, s'il n'a lieu que pour une seule chose tandis qu'on éprouve une disette d'une autre, ces nouveaux besoins, cette nécessité, donnent l'idée des échanges. Dès lors les relations morales se compliquent et se multiplient."

9. See, however, Hont, *Politics in Commercial Society*.

10. For further examination of discussions of the division of labour in the early nineteenth century, see Sonenscher, *The Romans, the Germans and the Moderns*, ch. 3.

Chapter II. Capitalism and the History of Political Thought

1. On republicanism, see J.G.A. Pocock, *The Machiavellian Moment: Florentine Political Thought and the Atlantic Republican Tradition* [Princeton, NJ, Princeton UP, 1975], 2nd ed. (Princeton, NJ, Princeton UP, 2003), and the 3rd ed. introduced informatively by

Richard Whatmore (Princeton, NJ, Princeton UP, 2016). On the various origins of republicanism, see Eric Nelson, *The Hebrew Republic: Jewish Sources and the Transformation of European Thought* (Cambridge, MA, Harvard UP, 2010) and his earlier *The Greek Tradition in Republican Thought* (Cambridge, CUP, 2004). On liberty and republicanism, see Quentin Skinner, *Liberty before Liberalism* (Cambridge, CUP, 1998), and Philip Pettit, *Republicanism: A Theory of Freedom and Government* (Oxford, OUP, 1997). On representation and representative government, see Quentin Skinner, *Hobbes and Republican Liberty* (Cambridge, CUP, 2008); David Runciman, *Pluralism and the Personality of the State* (Cambridge, CUP, 1997); John Dunn, *Western Political Theory in the Face of the Future* (Cambridge, CUP, 1979), and Istvan Hont, *Jealousy of Trade: International Competition and the Nation-State in Historical Perspective* (Cambridge, MA, Harvard UP, 2005). On sovereignty and government, see Richard Tuck, *The Sleeping Sovereign: The Invention of Modern Democracy* (Cambridge, CUP, 2015) and his earlier *Philosophy and Government 1572–1651* (Cambridge, CUP, 1993). On human rights, see Lynn Hunt, *Inventing Human Rights: A History* (New York, Norton, 2007), and on modern democracy, see Jonathan Israel, *The Radical Enlightenment* (Oxford, OUP, 2001) together with his *A Revolution of the Mind: Radical Enlightenment and the Intellectual Origins of Modern Democracy* (Princeton, NJ, Princeton UP, 2010), and, for a different approach, John Dunn, *Setting the People Free: The Story of Democracy* (London, Atlantic Books, 2005).

2. On positive and negative liberty, see Isaiah Berlin, "Two Concepts of Liberty" [1958], in Isaiah Berlin, *Four Essays on Liberty* (Oxford, OUP, 1969).

3. On these individuals, see Rupert Emerson, *State and Sovereignty in Modern Germany* (New Haven, CT, Yale UP, 1928). On Marx and capitalism, see Karl Marx and Friedrich Engels, *The*

Communist Manifesto, ed. Gareth Stedman Jones (London, Penguin Books, 2002), and, on Weber, see Wilhelm Hennis, *Max Weber's Science of Man* [1995] (Newbury, UK, Threshold Press, 2000) and his *Max Weber's Central Question* [1997] (Newbury, UK, Threshold Press, 2000), alongside Peter Ghosh, *A Historian Reads Max Weber* (Wiesbaden, Harrassowitz Verlag, 2008) and his *Max Weber and the Protestant Ethic: Twin Histories* (Oxford, OUP, 2014).

Chapter III. Capitalism, War, and Debt

1. On this usage, see Michael Sonenscher, *Before the Deluge: Public Debt, Inequality, and the Intellectual Origins of the French Revolution* (Princeton, NJ, Princeton UP, 2005). Despite its title, both the history of the word "capitalism" and the subject of the division of the labour are absent from the huge and otherwise illuminating Thomas Piketty, *Capital and Ideology* (Cambridge, MA, Belknap Press of Harvard UP, 2020) and, more recently, his equally illuminating *Une brève histoire de l'égalité* (Paris, Seuil, 2021). See too Piketty, Symposium, on the former book, published in *Œconomia* 11 (2021). On *Kapital*, *Kapitalist*, and *Kapitalismus*, see the entries for these words by Marie-Elisabeth Hilger and Lucian Hölscher, in *Geschichtliche Grundbegriffe*, ed. Oscar Brunner, Werner Conze, and Reinhart Koselleck, 8 vols. (Stuttgart, Klett-Cotta, 1972–97), vol. 3 (1982): 399–454.

2. "Au point où sont venues les choses, dans les Pays-Bas, c'est un duel que l'affaire hollando-belge.

Non un duel par les armes: la diplomatie ne le permettrait pas, mais un duel commercial, économique et fiscal, où, sauf quelque subite péripétie, la victoire doit rester du côté des gros sacs, sinon du côté des gros bataillons, où Frédéric II prétendait qu'elle se fixait toujours. Or, les gros sacs ne sont pas aujourd'hui du côté de Léopold. Sans doute la Hollande ne compte plus, comme au temps de Jean de Witt, dix mille voiles et cent cinquante mille matelots; mais elle dispose d'une puissance dont la Grande-Bretagne a longtemps exercé le monopole. Cette puissance, c'est le capitalisme, et voilà comment elle l'a acquise.

"A l'époque de sa grande prospérité, la Hollande s'était non-seulement emparée du monopole des mers et du commerce, mais au milieu de sa richesse, elle avait contracté des habitudes d'ordre et d'économie qui devaient un jour lui réserver d'immenses ressources. Le commerce enrichissait toutes les classes de la nation; toutes accumulaient des capitaux, et bientôt, après avoir été l'intermédiaire de l'Europe avec les contrées lointaines, le peuple hollandais en devint le banquier. Il n'est pas une puissance qui n'ait eu recours à sa bourse, et les négociants d'Amsterdam sont devenus les *argentiers* de tous les souverains." Emile Morice, "Hollande et Belgique," in his *Révélations et pamphlets* (Paris, 1834), pp. 207–8.

3. Ibid., pp. 209–13.

4. Ibid., pp. 213–29.

Chapter IV. Capitalism, Royalism,
and the Social Question

1. "C'est une question bien importante, nullement résolue encore, que celle du commerce considéré sous le point de vue politique. Né des produits naturels dont il accroit la valeur vénale et facilite les placements, n'enfante-t-il pas, dans son extension et à son dernier terme, deux vices sociaux aussi ruineux que corrupteurs? D'une part, c'est la surabondance des producteurs sur les consommateurs, qui force à une infériorité de fabrication; d'une autre, c'est la substitution du commerce stérile de l'or à l'écoulement vivificateur des produits de l'agriculture et de l'industrie." Alphonse de Beauchamp and Armand François, comte d'Allonville,

Mémoires tirés des papiers d'un homme d'état, 13 vols. (Paris, 1828–38), 11:45.

2. "Je ne noterai pas davantage l'inégale balance des produits et des consommations; après des maux inévitables un juste équilibre pourra s'établir. Mais que dire de cette puissance nouvelle du capitalisme qui, née de commerce qu'elle ruine, a succédé, avec toute son immoralité, à la puissance si morale de la fructification du sol qu'elle opprime en en détournant ses capitaux. De cette puissance qui sacrifie l'avenir au présent, et le présent à l'individualité, cette lèpre contemporaine. Cette puissance égoïste, cosmopolite, qui s'empare de tout, ne produit rien et n'est intimement lié qu'à elle-même. Souveraine des souverains, qui ne peuvent sans elle ni faire la guerre ni demeurer en paix et qui s'enrichit également de leur prospérité et de leur ruine, des biens du peuple qu'elle partage, de leurs maux qu'elle accroît." Ibid., p. 46.

3. "Depuis qu'Adam Smith a dit: «*L'argent n'est autre chose que le mobile de la circulation*» il n'a plus été considéré par les économistes que comme signe représentatif de la richesse, et le crédit comme une richesse réelle. De là, la création des valeurs fictives également représentatives de cette même richesse. De là, les banques, les papiers-monnaies et l'agiotage, fruit de l'abondance des effets publics; enfin l'aristocratie de la Bourse et la ressources des emprunts, banqueroute déguisée, car la multiplication du signe en atténue la valeur; multiplication dont le résultat définitif sera probablement une grande catastrophe financière." Ibid., p. 47 (italics in original).

4. "En Angleterre il y a deux *pouvoirs*, parce qu'il y a deux sociétés.

"Il y a une société politique constituée ou monarchique, avec ses lois fondamentales, sa religion publique, son *pouvoir* unique, ses distinctions sociales permanents.

"Il y a une société de commerce la plus étendue qu'il y ait dans l'univers, car l'état est commerçant en Angleterre, et n'est proprement commerçant qu'en Angleterre. Dans cette dernière société, le *pouvoir* est nécessairement séparé du *pouvoir* de la société politique parce que dans celle-ci le *pouvoir* est unique, dans l'autre il est collectif par la nature même de la société commerçante. En effet, ce n'est pas *une opposition d'intérêts particuliers et de volontés opposées qui a rendu nécessaire l'établissement de cette société*, mais une réunion libre d'intérêts communs et de volontés unanimes *qui l'a rendu possible*." Louis de Bonald, *Théorie du pouvoir politique et religieux dans la société civile* [1796], in Louis de Bonald, *Œuvres*, 2 vols. (Paris, Librairie d'Adrien Leclère, 1854), vol. 1, ch. 6, "Constitution d'Angleterre," pp. 450–51. On Bonald's thought, see Gérard Gengembre, "Entre archaïsme et modernité: Bonald, la contre-révolution et la littérature," *Revue d'histoire littéraire de la France* 90 (1990): 705–14, and his "Bonald ou l'esthétique sociale de la littérature," in *Romantismes: l'esthétisme en acte*, ed. Jean-Louis Cabanès (Paris, Presses Universitaires de Paris Ouest, 2009), pp. 143–54, as well as Flavien Bertran de Balanda, "Contre-révolution ou contre-subversion? Le sens rétabli selon Louis de Bonald, une métaphysique sémantique de la régénération sociale," in *Les mots du politique 1815–1848*, ed. Aude Déruelle and Corinne Legoy (Paris, Classiques Garnier, 2021), pp. 31–46.

On the phrase *société de commerce* in the first translation, by the poet Jean-Antoine Roucher, of Smith's term "commercial society," see Adam Smith, *Recherches sur la nature et les causes de la richesse des nations*, 4 vols. (Paris, 1790), 1:46: "C'est en vivant ainsi que chaque homme devient une sorte de marchand, et la société entière, une société de commerce." In the second, 1802, translation by Germain Garnier, the phrase became *une société commerçante*. "Ainsi chaque homme subsiste d'échanges ou devient une espèce de marchand, et la société elle-même est proprement une société commerçante" (Smith, *Recherches*, 1:46). Bonald's use of the earlier phrase is mentioned in Lucien Jaume, *Tocqueville: The Aristocratic Sources of Liberty* [2008] (Princeton, NJ, Princeton UP, 2013), p. 98, n. 11.

5. Thomas Hobbes, *Elements of Law Natural & Politic* [1640], ed. Ferdinand Tönnies, introduced by M. M. Goldsmith (London, Cass, 1969), pt. 2, ch. 8, sec. 7, pp. 173–74.

6. Ibid., p. 451.

7. The passage is quoted by Bonald in a footnote on pp. 452–53 of his text. On Montesquieu's so-called prophecy, see Sonenscher, *Before the Deluge*, pp. 44–46.

8. Reinhart Koselleck, *Critique and Crisis: Enlightenment and the Pathogenesis of Modern Society* [1959] (Cambridge, MA, MIT Press; Leamington Spa, UK, Berg Publishers, 1988).

9. On words that end in -ism, see Cesare Cuttica, "*To Use or Not to Use . . . The Intellectual Historian and the Isms:* A Survey and a Proposal," *Etudes Epistémè* 13 (2013), Varia, http://episteme.revues.org/268; Jussi Kurunmäki and Jani Marjanen, "A Rhetorical View of Isms: An Introduction," *Journal of Political Ideologies* 23 (2018): 241–55, and their "Isms, Ideologies and Setting the Agenda for Public Debate," in the same issue, pp. 256–82, as well as Jani Marjanen, "Ism Concepts in Science and Politics," *Contributions to the History of Concepts* 13 (2018): v–ix, together with the further bibliography supplied there. Further discussion of the subject will appear in the final chapter of my *The Romans, the Germans and the Moderns*.

10. "Avec le malaise ou l'instabilité de la fortune privée, concorde le malaise encore plus pénétrant de la fortune sociale: et un mal nouveau, le *capitalisme*, insinuant et dangereux serpent, étouffe en ses plis et replis l'une et l'autre." Pons Louis Frédéric, marquis de Villeneuve, *De l'agonie de la France*, 2 vols [1835] 2nd ed. (Paris, 1839), 1:139–40, 168–69, 173 (here p. 139).

11. "Il faudrait enfin comprendre qu'en dehors des conditions parlementaires d'un pouvoir, il y a une question sociale à laquelle il faut satisfaire. . . . Un gouvernement a toujours tort lorsqu'il n'a que des fins de non-recevoir à opposer à des gens qui demandent du pain." *La Quotidienne*, 28 November 1831, cited in Jean-Baptiste Duroselle, *Les débuts du catholicisme social en France (1822–1870)* (Paris, PUF, 1951), p. 201; see too Robert Castel, *Les métamorphoses de la question sociale* [1995] (Paris, Gallimard, 2013), p. 394.

Chapter V. Capitalism and the Right to Work

1. "Prolétaire, réjouis-toi, ton affranchissement s'avance. Il est sur, il est certain. Pourquoi? Parce que les douleurs qui t'assiègent, tu en connais la cause et le remède. Placé que tu es au-dessus du fait par l'ideal que tu as incarné, tu as conçu une vie supérieure à celle que le capitalisme t'a fait, et cherche à te prolonger. Prolétaire, tu n'es pas seulement républicain, tu es socialiste, socialiste comme l'étaient ou le sont Saint-Simon, Fourier, Robert Owen, Pierre Leroux, Louis Blanc, Proudhon, etc. Tu comprends, comme eux, la solidarité humaine, l'association. Tu raisonnes du travail, du capital; tu parles sciences, art. Tu sais ce que vaut un homme." Joseph Pierre Bazile Robert (Robert du Var), *Histoire de la classe ouvrière depuis l'esclave jusqu'au prolétaire de nos jours*, 4 vols. (Paris, 1845–47), 4:513.

2. "Le capital est un levier avec lequel l'industrie et le commerce remue le monde. Brisez le levier dans la main du riche qui le tenait; divisez-le entre tous; que ferez-vous de cet atome de levier, avec cette goutte d'eau d'une mer immense qui, ainsi divisée, ne ferait pas tourner un moulin de cartes; car, ne l'oubliez pas, la richesse divisée c'est la pauvreté universelle." Louis Bonnardet, "Rapport sur le concours ouvert sur l'éloge de Benjamin Delessert," *Mémoires de l'Académie Royale des Sciences, Belles-Lettres et*

Arts de Lyon, Section des Lettres, vol. 2 (Lyon, 1846), p. 279. Note that the date of publication is either a typographical slip or a reference to the date of an earlier award ceremony because the content of the report indicates clearly that it was published in 1848 as a written version of an earlier speech.

3. "Une lutte récemment engagée entre Lamartine et L. Blanc a donné naissance à un nouveau mot, le *capitalisme*. Ce n'est pas au capital, s'écrie ce dernier, que nous avons déclaré la guerre, mais au *capitalisme*; c'est-à-dire, sans doute, aux capitalistes. Je le crois parbleu bien, et nous le savons de reste. Nous savons bien que ce n'est pas le capital qui nous gêne mais le capitaliste. Mais M. L. Blanc voudrait-il bien nous dire ce que deviendrait le capital sans capitalistes. Ce que devient, je le suppose, l'eau quand on supprime le réservoir qui la contient." Ibid., p. 282, n. 1. On the rivalry, but also the similarity, between Lamartine and Louis Blanc, see Dominique Dupart, *Le lyrisme démocratique ou la naissance de l'éloquence romantique chez Lamartine 1834–1849* (Paris, Champion, 2019), pp. 22, 25.

4. The two quotations are both from a letter by Lamartine to Emile de Girardin, 24 December 1844, in Alphonse de Lamartine, *Correspondance (1807–1852)*, ed. Valentine de Lamartine, 6 vols., vol. 6 (Paris, 1875), p. 148.

5. Charles Fourier, *The Theory of the Four Movements* [1822], ed. Gareth Stedman Jones and Ian Patterson (Cambridge, CUP, 1996), pp. 262–63.

6. See, particularly, François Ewald, *Histoire de l'état providence* (Paris, Grasset, 1996) and his earlier, larger, thesis entitled *L'état providence* (Grasset, 1986).

7. "Quant à l'organisation du travail, c'est-à-dire à une intervention souveraine de l'état dans les rapports de l'ouvrier avec le maître, le capital avec le salaire, intervention par laquelle l'état règlerait la production, la consommation, et gouvernerait le capital et le

salaire, nous confessons que notre intelligence ne s'est jamais
élevée jusqu'à la compréhension de ce gouvernement de la liberté
par l'arbitraire, et de la concurrence par le monopole." Alphonse
de Lamartine, "Du droit au travail et de l'organisation du travail"
[1844], in Alphonse de Lamartine, *Œuvres, Etudes oratoires et politiques*, 2 vols. (Paris, 1849), 2:185.

8. "Qu'entendez-vous, leur dirons-nous par l'*organisation du
travail*? Est-ce le rétablissement des corporations exclusives
d'ouvriers, des *jurandes* et des *maitrises*, sortes de cadres légaux où
on ne laissait entrer qu'un certain nombre d'ouvriers, de peur
qu'un plus grand nombre ne dépassât les besoins de la profession
et ne se fît à soi-même concurrence? Mais qui ne voit qu'en garan-
tissant ainsi le travail pour ceux qui sont dans les cadres, vous
l'interdisez à ceux qui sont dehors, et que vous ruinez ainsi d'une
main le travail que vous garantissez de l'autre? La révolution toute
entière a été faite pour que tous les emplois fussent librement accessibles à tous les citoyens; et vous commenceriez par déclarer le
travail, le salaire et le pain accessibles seulement à ceux-ci, inacces-
sibles à ceux-là? Vous avez renversé l'aristocratie et la féodalité au
sommet de votre société, et vous rétablirez l'aristocratie du travail
et la féodalité du salaire aux plus bas étages de votre ordre social?
Vous avez détruit la noblesse des rangs, et vous recréeriez la noblesse des outils? Vous avez conquis la liberté civile et politique,
et vous déclareriez l'arbitraire et l'esclavage des professions? Mais
ce serait la contre-révolution la plus stupide! Ce serait avoir deux
principes de gouvernement contradictoires dans le même état. Ce
serait couper la nation en deux. Ce serait déclarer que ce qui est
vrai en haut est mensonge en bas, et que pendant que la partie
politique et propriétaire du pays sera gouvernée par la liberté, la
partie ouvrière et prolétaire sera gouvernée par l'arbitraire. C'est-
à-dire, ce serait déclarer une nation de citoyens et une nation
d'esclaves. Mais à quoi bon le discuter? Il suffit de défier qui que

ce soit d'accomplir ce suicide de liberté. S'il y avait des hommes assez insensés pour le tenter, où serait le peuple pour le souffrir?" Ibid., pp. 186–87.

9. "La fraternité, en définition, consiste à faire un sacrifice pour autrui, à travailler pour autrui. Quand elle est libre, spontanée, volontaire, je la conçois, et j'y applaudis. J'admire d'autant plus le sacrifice qu'il est plus entier. Mais quand on pose au sein d'une société ce principe, que la fraternité sera imposé par la loi, c'est-à-dire, en bon français, que la répartition des fruits du travail sera faite législativement, sans égard pour les droits du travail lui-même, qui peut dire dans quelle mesure ce principe agira, de quelle forme un caprice du législateur peut le revêtir, dans quelles institutions un décret peut du soir au lendemain l'incarner? Or, je demande si, à ces conditions, une société peut exister?" Frédéric Bastiat, "Justice et fraternité" [1848], in his *Œuvres économiques*, ed. Florin Aftalion (Paris, PUF, 1983), p. 114. See also his "Un économiste à M. Lamartine à l'occasion de son écrit intitulé *Du droit au travail*," *Journal des économistes* 10 (1845): 209–23. On the wider discussion, see Yves Breton, "Les économistes, le pouvoir politique et l'ordre social en France entre 1830 et 1851," *Histoire, Economie, Société* 4 (1985): 233–52.

10. For an example of the association, see Keith Tribe, *The Economy of the Word: Language, History, and Economics* (Oxford, OUP, 2015), p. 9, n. 18. On Louis Blanc, see Francis Démier, ed., *Un socialiste en république: Louis Blanc* (Paris, Créaphis, 2005), notably the chapter by Démier himself, and Leo Loubère, *Louis Blanc: His Life and His Contribution to the Rise of French Jacobin-Socialism* (Evanston, IL, Northwestern UP, 1961).

11. "Vous reprochez aux socialistes de vouloir supprimer le capital et le capitaliste. Bêtise! Car vous confondez ici ce que jamais les socialistes ne confondirent, et vous leur prêtez votre propre ignorance. Dans tout système, le capital, sachez-le bien, est

regardé comme absolument indispensable à l'œuvre de la production industrielle ou agricole. Mais, loin de perdre son utilité en passant du service d'un individu isolé au service de l'association, il se multiplie. Loin de périr, en se concentrant, il s'accroît. La suppression du *capitalisme* ne saurait donc être aucunement la suppression du *capital*. Rassembler les détachements épars d'une armée, est-ce la détruire?" Louis Blanc, *Le nouveau monde*, vols. 1–2 (1849), p. 34.

Chapter VII. Karl Marx—Capitalism, Communism, and the Division of Labour

1. Credit for the rediscovery of the term goes to Istvan Hont in a lecture entitled "Negative Community: The Natural Law Heritage from Pufendorf to Marx," given within the John M. Olin Program in the History of Political Culture, 1 February 1989. For later developments, see the introduction by Gareth Stedman Jones to his edition of Marx and Engels, *The Communist Manifesto*, pp. 162–76, and his *Karl Marx: Greatness and Illusion* (London, Allen Lane, 2016), pp. 174–80 (here, however, without the concept of a negative community).

2. United States Reports, *Cases Adjudged in the Supreme Court at October Term, 1895* (New York, 1896), Geer v. Connecticut, p. 525, citing Robert Joseph Pothier, *Traité du droit de domaine de propriété*, 2 vols. [1762] (Paris, 1772), vol. 1, § 21, pp. 23–24: "Les premiers hommes eurent d'abord en commun toutes les choses que Dieu avait données au genre humain. Cette communauté n'était pas une communauté positive, telle que celle qui est entre plusieurs particuliers qui ont en commun le domaine d'une chose dans laquelle ils ont chacun leur part ; c'était une communauté que ceux qui ont traité de ces matières appellent *communauté négative*, laquelle consistait en ce que ces choses qui étaient communes à

tous n'appartenaient pas plus à aucun d'eux, qu'aux autres, et qu'aucun ne pouvait empêcher un autre de prendre dans ces choses communes ce qu'il jugeait à propos d'y prendre pour s'en servir dans ses besoins. Pendant qu'il s'en servait les autres devaient la lui laisser, mais après qu'il avait cessé de s'en servir, si la chose n'était pas de celles qui se consument par l'usage qu'on en fait, cette chose rentrait dans la communauté négative, et un autre pouvait s'en servir de même.

"Le genre humain s'étant multiplié, les hommes partagèrent entr'eux la terre et la plupart des choses qui étaient sur sa surface, ce qui échut à chacun d'eux commença à lui appartenir privativement à tous les autres. C'est l'origine du droit de propriété.

"Tout n'entra pas dans ce partage. Plusieurs choses restèrent et plusieurs sont encore aujourd'hui demeurées dans cet ancien état de communauté négative."

3. Proudhon's notes on Pothier can be found in Bibliothèque nationale de France, *Nouvelles acquisitions françaises*, 18258, cahier 12, "Notes sur Pothier. "The earth was *given* to the human race," he wrote in a comment on Pothier's assertion, "why did I not get anything? God laid out nature at my feet, but I have nowhere to rest my head." ("La terre a été *donné* au genre humain, pourquoi donc n'ai-je rien reçu? Dieu a mis la nature sous mes pieds, et je n'ai pas où reposer ma tête.") I owe the quotation to Edward Castleton.

4. Pierre Joseph Proudhon, *What Is Property?* [1840], ed. Donald R. Kelley and Bonnie G. Smith (Cambridge, CUP, 1994), p. 195 (which is also where the phrase "negative community" occurs). For the French original and a helpful introduction, see Proudhon, *Qu'est-ce que la propriété?*, ed. Robert Damien and Edward Castleton (Paris, Livre de Poche, 2009); see pp. 406–7 for the passages quoted here.

5. Ibid., p. 211.

6. The intellectual origins of Marx's concept of the proletariat are described in Sonenscher, *The Romans, the Germans and the Moderns*, ch. 3.

7. Georg Simmel, *Fundamental Problems of Sociology (Individual and Society)* [1917], in *The Sociology of Georg Simmel*, ed. Kurt H. Wolff (New York, Free Press, 1950), pp. 80–81. For an illuminating examination of this concept of individualism and its bearing on Simmel's thought, see Efraim Podoksik, "Georg Simmel: Three Forms of Individualism and Historical Understanding," *New German Critique* 10 (2010): 119–45, and, more recently, his *Georg Simmel and German Culture: Unity, Variety and Modern Discontents* (Cambridge, CUP, 2021).

8. Friedrich Schleiermacher, *Soliloquies* [1800], ed. Horace Leland Friess (New York, Columbia UP, 1926), pp. 30–31. On this aspect of Schleiermacher's thought, see Frederick Beiser, "Schleiermacher's Ethics," in *The Cambridge Companion to Friedrich Schleiermacher*, ed. Jacqueline Mariña (Cambridge, CUP, 2005), pp. 53–71 (especially pp. 60–61), and, recently, Ruth Jackson Ravenscroft, *The Veiled God: Friedrich Schleiermacher's Theology of Finitude* (Leiden, Brill, 2019), pp. 100–105.

9. Ludwig Feuerbach, *The Essence of Christianity* [1841], trans. Marian Evans [George Eliot] (New York, 1855), p. 7. On this aspect of Marx's thought, see Michael Quante, "Positive Liberty as Realizing the Essence of Man," in *Positive Freedom, Past, Present, and Future*, ed. John Christman (Cambridge, CUP, 2022), pp. 28–44.

10. On Cieszkowski, see the fine study by André Liebich, *Between Ideology and Utopia* (Dordrecht, 1979), and, helpfully, Lawrence Dickey, "Saint-Simonian Industrialism as the End of History: August Cieszkowski and the Teleology of Universal History," in *Apocalypse Theory and the Ends of the World*, ed. Malcolm Bull (Oxford, Blackwell, 1995), pp. 159–99. See too Christophe Bouton,

"L'histoire de l'avenir. Cieszkowski lecteur de Hegel," *Revue Germanique Internationale* 8 (2008): 77–92; Andrej Walicki, *Philosophy and Romantic Nationalism: The Case of Poland* (Oxford, OUP, 1982), pp. 127–51, 295–307, and his *Russia, Poland, and Universal Regeneration* (Notre Dame, IN, U of Notre Dame Press, 1991), pp. 73–106; as well as Leszek Kolakowski, *Main Currents of Marxism*, 3 vols. (Oxford, Clarendon Press, 1978), 1:85–88. For English translations of Cieszkowski's works, see August Cieszkowski, *Selected Writings*, ed. André Liebich (Cambridge, CUP, 1979), and Lawrence S. Stepelevich, ed., *The Young Hegelians: An Anthology* (Cambridge, CUP, 1983), pp. 55–89.

11. For these, see the introduction by Gareth Stedman Jones to Marx and Engels, *The Communist Manifesto*, pp. 1–184, and p. 219 for the phrase quoted from the *Manifesto* itself.

Chapter VIII. Adam Smith—Capitalism, Utility, and Justice

1. August Oncken, "The Consistency of Adam Smith," *Economic Journal* 7 (1897): 443–50; and "Das Adam Smith–Problem," *Zeitschrift fur Sozialwissenschaft* 1 (1898): 25–33, 101–8, 276–87.

2. These are set out very clearly in Laurence Dickey, "Historicizing the 'Adam Smith Problem': Conceptual, Historiographical and Textual Issues," *Journal of Modern History* 58 (1986): 579–609. For further discussion, see Tribe, *The Economy of the Word*, pp. 139–62, and his "'Das Adam Smith Problem' and the Origins of Modern Smith Scholarship," *History of European Ideas* 34 (2008): 514–25, and, more recently, "The 'System of Natural Liberty': Natural Order in the *Wealth of Nations*," *History of European Ideas* 47 (2021): 573–83, as well as Leonidas Montes, *Adam Smith in Context* (Basingstoke, UK, Macmillan, 2004), pp. 15–56. For a recent indication of the problem's ongoing salience, see Denis

Baranger, *Penser la loi. Essai sur le législateur des temps modernes* (Paris, Gallimard, 2018), pp. 291–302.

3. See Istvan Hont and Michael Ignatieff, "Needs and Justice in the *Wealth of Nations*: An Introductory Essay," in *Wealth and Virtue: The Shaping of Political Economy in the Scottish Enlightenment*, ed. Istvan Hont and Michael Ignatieff (Cambridge, CUP, 1983), pp. 1–44; Samuel Fleischacker, *On Adam Smith's* Wealth of Nations: *A Philosophical Companion* (Princeton, NJ, Princeton UP, 2004), pp. 200–202, 209–26; Samuel Fleischacker, *A Short History of Distributive Justice* (Cambridge, MA, Harvard UP, 2004), pp. 17–18, 26–40; J. R. Otteson, "The Recurring 'Adam Smith Problem,'" *History of Philosophy Quarterly* 17 (2000): 51–74; and Knud Haakonssen and Donald Winch, "The Legacy of Adam Smith," in *The Cambridge Companion to Adam Smith*, ed. Knud Haakonssen (Cambridge, CUP, 2006), pp. 366–94.

4. Dugald Stewart, *An Account of the Life and Writings of Adam Smith* [1793], in *Biographical Memoirs of Adam Smith, William Robertson and Thomas Reid*, ed. Sir William Hamilton (Edinburgh, 1858), p. 12.

5. James Mackintosh, *A General View of the Progress of Ethical Philosophy* [1831] (Philadelphia, 1834), p. 12.

6. Ibid., p. 13.

7. James Reddie, *Inquiries Elementary and Historical in the Science of Law* (London, 1840), p. 16. Unless otherwise stated, reference will always be to the first edition.

8. Ibid., p. 10.

9. Ibid., p. 14.

10. Reddie, *Inquiries* (2nd ed.), p. 223.

11. Ibid., p. 224.

12. Ibid., 224–25. The same point about Kant as the first to make a sharp distinction between morality and the law was made by the French law professor William Bélime in his *Philosophie du*

droit, ou cours d'introduction à la science du droit, 2 vols. (Paris, 1855), 1:10: "C'est au surplus un des principaux services de Kant que d'avoir le premier tracé d'une main ferme cette importante distinction."

13. Reddie, *Inquiries* (2nd ed.), p. 225. The passage was taken from Savigny's *System des Heutigen Römischen Rechts,* which began to appear in 1840. See Friedrich Carl von Savigny, *System des Heutigen Römischen Rechts* (Berlin, 1840), §52.

14. Reddie, *Inquiries* (2nd ed.), p. 226.

15. Jean-Jacques Rousseau, *Of the Social Contract,* in Jean-Jacques Rousseau, *Collected Writings,* ed. Roger D. Masters and Christopher Kelly, 14 vols. (Hanover, NH, University Press of New England, 1987–2007), vol. 4, bk. 3, ch. 4, p. 174.

Chapter IX. Georg Wilhelm Friedrich Hegel— Civil Society and the State

1. See, however, Erk Volkmar Heyen, ed., *Formation und Transformation des Verwaltungswissens in Frankreich und Deutschland (18./19. Jh.) / Formation et transformation du savoir administratif en France et en Allemagne (18e/19e s)* (Baden-Baden, Nomos, 1989), particularly the chapters by Thomas R. Osborne and David F. Lindenfeld. See too Riccardo Soliani, ed., *Economic Thought and Institutional Change in France and Italy (1789–1914)* (Heidelberg, Springer, 2017), and, for a helpful historical illustration, the recent article by Nicolas Barreyre and Claire Lemercier, "The Unexceptional State: Rethinking the State in the Nineteenth Century," *American Historical Review* 126 (2021): 481–503.

2. On Hegel and Steuart, see Paul Chamley, "Les origines de la pensée économique de Hegel," *Hegel Studien* 3 (1965): 225–61, and his "Notes de lectures relatives à Smith, Steuart et Hegel," *Revue d'économie politique* 77 (1967): 857–78. On Steuart and public debt,

see Ramón Tortajada, ed., *The Economics of Sir James Steuart* (London, Routledge, 1999), and Sonenscher, *Before the Deluge*, pp. 24–26, 58–64, 256–58.

3. Georg Wilhelm Friedrich Hegel, *Elements of the Philosophy of Right* [1821] (Cambridge, CUP, 1991), §205, p. 237 (henceforth Hegel, *EPR*, followed by the lemma and page numbers).

4. Hegel, *EPR*, §303, p. 343.

5. Hegel, *EPR*, §299, p. 338 (italics in original).

6. Hegel, *EPR*, §299, pp. 337–39.

7. The analogy to shoemaking can be found in Archives nationales de France (henceforth AN) 284 AP 4, dossier 5: "Since it is not the nation as a body, since it is not every citizen who goes about producing everything needed to meet his needs, it can be said quite truthfully that all the work undertaken in society is *representative*. The rich, delicate lady living in the most luxurious of cities whose daily occupations are the furthest removed from those of the humblest artisan should know that her existence is very highly based on representation and that what he does amounts to her most essential capital. She should not therefore despise someone entrusted with her commission since, if the worker who supplies her with slippers stopped working, the result would be that she would have to do it herself, and would do it a great deal less well and at a great deal more cost." ("Puisque ce n'est pas la nation en corps, puisque ce n'est pas tout citoyen qui vaque à la production de tout ce qui sert à remplir ses besoins, on peut dire avec vérité que tous les travaux de la société sont *représentatif*. Il faut que la femme riche et délicate qui dans la ville la plus luxueuse se trouve par ses occupations journalières la plus éloignée du travail du plus grossier artisan sache cependant que son existence est fort représentative et [que] son capital essentiel est ce qu'il fait. Elle ne doit pas mépriser son chargé de procuration, car si l'ouvrier qui la fournit des souliers ne travaillait pas, il

suivrait bien qu'elle y travaillerait elle-même et qu'elle ferait beaucoup plus mal et qu'il lui coûterait beaucoup plus cher.")

8. AN 284 AP 2, dossier 13 (sheet headed "travail") (italics in
original).

9. See Emmanuel-Joseph Sieyès, *Political Writings*, ed. Michael
Sonenscher (Indianapolis, IN, Hackett, 2003), p. 48.

10. AN 284 AP 5, dossier 32 (sheet headed *onéologie*). The original French passage runs as follows (I have modernised the spell-
ing): "La richesse proprement dite se compose de toutes les valeurs existantes; mais l'onéologie jusqu'à présent ne considère que
les valeurs vénales. L'aisance, le bien-être, la jouissance, en un mot,
tiennent à beaucoup d'autres biens que les richesses vénales et
même que les richesses aussi nombreuses qui se consomment sans
avoir été vendues. Dans cette seule observation, on voit déjà que
l'onéologie peut recevoir une étendue dont on ne s'est pas encore
avisé. Le travail que chacun s'applique directement et les jouissances particulières, communes et publiques, ouvrent un champ
immense d'éléments de bonheur qui n'ont point encore été l'objet
de cette étude. Un bon état social combinerait les choses de
manière que les jouissances morales et physiques qui ne se ven-
dent point entreraient pour une portion considérable dans le bien
être de chaque individu. L'industrie et l'action humaines me para-
issent bien resserrés quand on ne considère que leur produit vénal
(voir le tableau analytique que j'ai fait il y a plus de 40 ans de
l'universalité de la jouissance humaine). Le spectacle d'une société
humaine sous le rapport du bien être générale me semble bien
misérable quand on ne représente les individus qui la composent
que comme une multitude d'agents ou d'instruments des seules
productions vénales. Comme si une association politique n'était
que la formation d'une grande manufacture, où trois classes
d'individus, des rentiers oisifs, des entrepreneurs actifs et des instruments laborieux se font constamment une guerre sourde pour

avoir la plus grande part au produit vénal. La production et la consommation sont des choses corrélatives, quoique rarement égales;
les richesses destinés à être vendues; celles mêmes qui en seraient
susceptibles, quoique ne l'étant pas, ne composent dans le mouvement général que la plus petite portion de la consommation et de
la production. L'onéologie n'a donc pas reçu toute l'extension
qu'elle doit avoir comme *science politique*. Je m'étais occupé de
cette vue, avec beaucoup de suite, en 1774 et années suivantes. Elle
m'avoit dirigé dans le projet d'établissement des fêtes publiques
que j'ai donné au comité d'instruction publique en 1793 etc. *Fata
negarunt*."

11. AN 284 AP 3, dossier 13.

Chapter X. David Ricardo—Public Debt and Comparative Advantage

1. For a helpful and clear summary, see Helen Paul, "David Ri-
cardo," in *Great Economic Thinkers*, ed. Jonathan Conlin (London,
Reaktion Books, 2018), pp. 40–53, and, for broad overviews, see
Heinz D. Kurz and Neri Salvadori, eds., *The Elgar Companion to
David Ricardo* (Cheltenham, UK, Edward Elgar, 2015), particularly
pp. 65–77, and, more recently, Ryan Walter, *Before Method and
Models: The Political Economy of Malthus and Ricardo* (Oxford,
OUP, 2021). For two comprehensive and well-documented ac-
counts that complement the more summary argument set out
here, see Gilbert Faccarello, "A Calm Investigation into Mr Ri-
cardo's Principles of International Trade," *European Journal of the
History of Economic Thought* 22 (2015): 754–90, and, with more of
a focus on Ricardo on money, Alain Béraud and Gilbert Faccarello, "'Nous marchons sur un autre terrain': The Reception of
David Ricardo in the French Language: Episodes from a Complex
History," in *The Reception of David Ricardo in Continental Europe*

and Japan, ed. Gilbert Faccarello and Masashi Izumo (London, Routledge, 2014), pp. 10–75.

2. See, recently, Paul Cheney, "István Hont, the Cosmopolitan Theory of Commercial Globalization, and Twenty-First-Century Capitalism," *Modern Intellectual History*, 2021, pp. 1–29: doi: 10.1017/S147924432100007X.

3. David Ricardo, *The Principles of Political Economy and Taxation* (London, 1817), ch. 27, p. 361.

4. Ibid., p. 362.

Chapter XI. Lorenz von Stein—Public Debt and Public Administration

1. On Stein, see Felix Gilbert, *History: Choice and Commitment* (Cambridge, MA, Harvard UP, 1977), pp. 411–21. More generally, see Pasquale Pasquino, "Introduction to Lorenz von Stein," *Economy and Society* 10 (1981): 1–6; Olivier Jouanjan, "Lorenz von Stein et les contradictions du mouvement constitutionnel révolutionnaire (1789–1794)," *Annales historiques de la révolution française* 328 (2002): 171–91; Peter Koslowski, ed., *The Theory of Ethical Economy in the Historical School* (Berlin, Springer Verlag, 1995); and Norbert Waszek, "L'état de droit social chez Lorenz von Stein," in *Figures de l'état de droit: Le Rechtsstaat dans l'histoire intellectuelle et constitutionnelle de l'Allemagne*, ed. Olivier Jouanjan (Strasbourg, Presses universitaires de Strasbourg, 2001), pp. 193–217.

2. Lorenz von Stein, *Geschichte der sozialen Bewegung in Frankreich von 1789 bis auf unsere Tage* (Leipzig, 1850), pt. 3, pp. 218–19 (italics in original), cited in Ernst-Wolfgang Böckenförde, "Lorenz von Stein, théoricien du mouvement de l'état et de la société vers l'état social," in his *Le droit, l'état et la constitution démocratique* (Paris, L.G.D.J.; Brussels, Bruylant, 2000), p. 149. See too Lorenz Stein, *Le concept de société*, trans. Marc Béghin, ed. Norbert Waszek

(Grenoble, ELLUG, 2002). For English-language versions of some of Böckenförde's publications, see his *State, Society and Liberty: Studies in Political Theory and Constitutional Law* (Oxford, Berg, 1991), and the two collections of his articles entitled *Constitutional and Political Theory*, ed. Mirjam Künkler and Tine Stein (Oxford, OUP, 2017), and *Religion, Law, and Democracy: Selected Writings*, ed. Mirjam Künkler and Tine Stein (Oxford, OUP, 2020).

3. Stein, *Le concept de société*. Originally published as *Geschichte der sozialen Bewegung in Frankreich, von 1789 bis auf unsere Tage* (1850). Reference in what follows is to the Waszek edition, here indicated simply by "Stein" and the page number, as in this case, Stein, p. 63.

4. Stein, pp. 79–80.

5. Stein, pp. 101–2.

6. Stein, pp. 80–81, 145.

7. Stein, pp. 107–10; see pp. 190 and 196 for the phrase "acquisitive society."

8. Stein, pp. 121–225

9. Stein, pp. 106–7. On the administrative aspect of Stein's thought, see Stedman Jones, *Karl Marx*, pp. 140–41.

10. The passage (from the 1871 edition of Stein's textbook on public finance, *Lehrbuch der Finanzwissenschaft*, p. 666) is quoted by Carl-Ludwig Holtfrerich, *Government Debt in the Economic Thought of the Long 19th Century* (Discussion Paper 2013/4, School of Business and Economics, Freie Universität, Berlin, 2013), pp. 17–18. See also his "Public Debt in Post-1850 German Economic Thought vis-à-vis the Pre-1850 British Classical School," *German Economic Review* 15 (2013): 62–83.

11. The phrases are quoted in Maurice Block, *Les progrès de la science économique depuis Adam Smith*, 2 vols. (Paris, Guillaumin, 1890), 1:403. Compare to Piketty, *Une brève histoire de l'égalité*, pp. 342–48.

12. Stein, p. 202 (italics in original).

Chapter XII. Conclusion

1. For a helpful description, see Maximillian E. Novak, "Robinson Crusoe and Economic Utopia," *Kenyon Review* 25 (1963): 474–90.

2. "L'homme est né libre, et partout il est dans les fers. Tel se croit le maitre des autres, qui ne laisse pas d'être plus esclave qu'eux. Comment ce changement s'est-il fait? Je l'ignore. Qu'est-ce qui peut le rendre légitime? Je crois pouvoir résoudre cette question." Jean-Jacques Rousseau, *Du contrat social*, bk. 1, ch. 1. I have relied on the English translation published as John James Rousseau, *An Inquiry into the Nature of the Social Contract, or Principles of Political Right* (Dublin, 1791), p. 3. For discussion of the division of labour in Rousseau's thought, see Michael Sonenscher, *Jean-Jacques Rousseau: The Division of Labour, the Politics of the Imagination and the Concept of Federal Government* (Leiden, Brill, 2019), pp. 51–85.

BIBLIOGRAPHY

Arrighi, Giovanni. *The Long Twentieth Century: Money, Power and the Origins of Our Times*. London, Verso, 1994.

———. "Capitalism and the Modern World System." *Review* (Fernand Braudel Center) 21 (1998): 113–29.

Balanda, Flavien Bertran de. "Contre-révolution ou contre-subversion? Le sens rétabli selon Louis de Bonald, une métaphysique sémantique de la régénération sociale." In *Les mots du politique 1815–1848*, ed. Aude Déruelle and Corinne Legoy, pp. 31–46. Paris, Classiques Garnier, 2021.

Baranger, Denis. *Penser la loi. Essai sur le législateur des temps modernes*. Paris, Gallimard, 2018.

Barreyre, Nicolas, and Claire Lemercier. "The Unexceptional State: Rethinking the State in the Nineteenth Century." *American Historical Review* 126 (2021): 481–503.

Bastiat, Frédéric. "Un économiste à M. Lamartine à l'occasion de son écrit intitulé *Du droit au travail*." *Journal des économistes* 10 (1845): 209–23.

———. "Justice et fraternité" [1848]. In his *Œuvres économiques*, ed. Florin Aftalion. Paris, PUF 1983.

Beauchamp, Alphonse de, and Armand François, comte d'Allonville. *Mémoires tirés des papiers d'un homme d'état*. 13 vols. Paris, 1828–38.

Beiser, Frederick. "Schleiermacher's Ethics." In *The Cambridge Companion to Friedrich Schleiermacher*, ed. Jacqueline Mariña, pp. 53–71. Cambridge, CUP, 2005.

Bélime, William. *Philosophie du droit, ou cours d'introduction à la science du droit*. 2 vols. Paris, 1855.

Benoit, Joseph. *Belgicismes ou les vices de langage et de prononciation les plus communs en Belgique corrigés d'après l'Académie et les meilleurs écrivains*. Antwerp, 1857.

Béraud, Alain, and Gilbert Faccarello. "'Nous marchons sur un autre terrain': The Reception of David Ricardo in the French Language: Episodes from a Complex History." In *The Reception of David Ricardo in Continental Europe and Japan*, ed. Gilbert Faccarello and Masashi Izumo, pp. 10–75. London, Routledge, 2014.

Berg, Maxine, ed. *Writing the History of the Global*. Oxford, OUP, 2013.

Berg, Maxine. "Commodity Frontiers: Concepts and History." *Journal of Global History* 16 (2021): 1–5, doi:10.1017/S1740022821000036.

Berlin, Isaiah. "Two Concepts of Liberty" [1958]. In Isaiah Berlin, *Four Essays on Liberty*. Oxford, OUP, 1969.

Blanc, Louis. *Le nouveau monde*. Vols. 1–2. 1849.

———. *Organisation du travail* [1839]. 9th ed. 1850.

Block, Maurice. *Les progrès de la science économique depuis Adam Smith*. 2 vols. Paris, Guillaumin, 1890.

Böckenförde, Ernst-Wolfgang. *State, Society and Liberty: Studies in Political Theory and Constitutional Law*. Oxford, Berg, 1991.

———. "Lorenz von Stein, théoricien du mouvement de l'état et de la société vers l'état social." In his *Le droit, l'état et la constitution démocratique*. Paris, L.G.D.J.; Brussels, Bruylant, 2000.

———. *Constitutional and Political Theory*. Ed. Mirjam Künkler and Tine Stein. Oxford, OUP, 2017.

————. *Religion, Law, and Democracy: Selected Writings.* Ed. Mirjam Künkler and Tine Stein. Oxford, OUP, 2020.

Bonald, Louis de. *Théorie du pouvoir politique et religieux dans la société civile* [1796]. In his *Œuvres*, 2 vols. Paris, Librairie d'Adrien Leclère, 1854.

Bonnardet, Louis. "Rapport sur le concours ouvert sur l'éloge de Benjamin Delessert." *Mémoires de l'Académie Royale des Sciences, Belles-Lettres et Arts de Lyon*, Section des Lettres, vol. 2. Lyon, 1846.

Bouton, Christophe. "L'histoire de l'avenir. Cieszkowski lecteur de Hegel." *Revue Germanique Internationale* 8 (2008): 77–92.

Braudel, Fernand. *Capitalism and Civilization.* 3 vols. London, Collins, 1982–85.

Breton, Yves. "Les économistes, le pouvoir politique et l'ordre social en France entre 1830 et 1851." *Histoire, Economie, Société* 4 (1985): 233–52.

Castel, Robert. *Les métamorphoses de la question sociale* [1995]. Paris, Gallimard, 2013.

Chamley, Paul. "Les origines de la pensée économique de Hegel." *Hegel Studien* 3 (1965): 225–61.

————. "Notes de lectures relatives à Smith, Steuart et Hegel." *Revue d'économie politique* 77 (1967): 857–78.

Cheney, Paul. "István Hont, the Cosmopolitan Theory of Commercial Globalization, and Twenty-First-Century Capitalism." *Modern Intellectual History*, 2021, pp. 1–29: doi: 10.1017/S147924432100007X.

Cieszkowski, August. *Selected Writings.* Ed. André Liebich. Cambridge, CUP, 1979.

Coleman, Charly. *The Spirit of French Capitalism: Economic Theology in the Age of Enlightenment.* Stanford, CA, Stanford UP, 2021.

Condorcet, Marie-Jean-Antoine-Nicolas, marquis de. *Sketch for a Historical Picture of the Progress of the Human Mind* [1793]. In *Condorcet: Selected Writings*, ed. Keith Michael Baker. Indianapolis, IN, Bobbs Merrill, 1976.

———. *Tableau historique des progrès de l'esprit humain: Projets, Esquisse, Fragments et Notes (1772–1794)*. Ed. Jean-Pierre Schandeler and Pierre Crépel. Paris, INED, 2004.

Conrad, Sebastian. *What Is Global History?* Princeton, NJ, Princeton UP, 2016.

Cuttica, Cesare. *"To Use or Not to Use* . . . The Intellectual Historian and the *Isms*: A Survey and a Proposal." *Etudes Epistémè* 13 (2013). Varia, http://episteme.revues.org/268.

Démier, Francis, ed. *Un socialiste en république: Louis Blanc*. Paris, Créaphis, 2005.

Dickey, Laurence. "Historicizing the 'Adam Smith Problem': Conceptual, Historiographical and Textual Issues." *Journal of Modern History* 58 (1986): 579–609.

———. "Saint-Simonian Industrialism as the End of History: August Cieszkowski and the Teleology of Universal History." In *Apocalypse Theory and the Ends of the World*, ed. Malcolm Bull, pp. 159–99. Oxford, Blackwell, 1995.

Dockès, Pierre. *Le capitalisme et ses rythmes*. 2 vols. Paris, Classiques Garnier, 2019–21.

Ducange, Jean-Numa, Razmig Keucheyan, and Stéphanie Roza, eds. *Histoire globale des socialismes*. Paris, PUF, 2021.

Dunn, John. *Western Political Theory in the Face of the Future*. Cambridge, CUP, 1979.

———. *Setting the People Free: The Story of Democracy*. London, Atlantic Books, 2005.

Dupart, Dominique. *Le lyrisme démocratique ou la naissance de l'éloquence romantique chez Lamartine 1834–1849*. Paris, Champion, 2019.

Duroselle, Jean-Baptiste. *Les débuts du catholicisme social en France (1822–1870)*. Paris, PUF, 1951.

Edwards, Andrew David, Peter Hill, and Juan Neves-Sarriegui. "Capitalism in Global History." *Past & Present* 249 (2020): e1–e32.

Emerson, Rupert. *State and Sovereignty in Modern Germany*. New Haven, CT, Yale UP, 1928.

Ewald, François. *L'état providence*. Paris, Grasset, 1986.

———. *Histoire de l'état providence*. Paris, Grasset, 1996.

Faccarello, Gilbert. "A Calm Investigation into Mr Ricardo's Principles of International Trade." *European Journal of the History of Economic Thought* 22 (2015): 754–90.

Federici, Silvia. *Caliban and the Witch: Women, the Body and Primitive Accumulation*. New York, Autonomedia, 2004.

Feuerbach, Ludwig, *The Essence of Christianity* [1841]. Trans. Marian Evans [George Eliot]. New York, 1855.

Fleischacker; Samuel. *On Adam Smith's* Wealth of Nations*: A Philosophical Companion*. Princeton, NJ, Princeton UP, 2004.

———. *A Short History of Distributive Justice*. Cambridge, MA, Harvard UP, 2004.

Fourier, Charles. *The Theory of the Four Movements* [1822]. Ed. Gareth Stedman Jones and Ian Patterson. Cambridge, CUP, 1996.

Gengembre, Gérard. "Entre archaïsme et modernité: Bonald, la contre-révolution et la littérature." *Revue d'histoire littéraire de la France* 90 (1990): 705–14.

———. "Bonald ou l'esthétique sociale de la littérature." In *Romantismes: l'esthétisme en acte*, ed. Jean-Louis Cabanès, pp. 143–54. Paris, Presses Universitaires de Paris Ouest, 2009.

Ghosh, Peter. *A Historian Reads Max Weber*. Wiesbaden, Harrassowitz Verlag, 2008.

———. *Max Weber and the Protestant Ethic: Twin Histories*. Oxford, OUP, 2014.

Gilbert, Felix. *History: Choice and Commitment.* Cambridge, MA, Harvard UP, 1977.

Grewe, Bernd-Stefan, and Karin Hofmeester, eds. *Luxury in Global Perspective: Objects and Practices, 1600–2000.* Cambridge, CUP, 2016.

Haakonssen, Knud, and Donald Winch. "The Legacy of Adam Smith." In *The Cambridge Companion to Adam Smith,* ed. Knud Haakonssen, pp. 366–94. Cambridge, CUP, 2006.

Hauser, Henri. "Kapitalismus." *Revue d'économie politique* 41 (1927): 1201–2.

Hegel, Georg Wilhelm Friedrich. *Elements of the Philosophy of Right* [1821]. Cambridge, CUP, 1991.

Hennis, Wilhelm. *Max Weber's Science of Man* [1995]. Newbury, UK, Threshold Press, 2000.

———. *Max Weber's Central Question* [1997]. Newbury, UK, Threshold Press, 2000.

Heyen, Erk Volkmar, ed. *Formation und Transformation des Verwaltungswissens in Frankreich und Deutschland (18./19. Jh.) / Formation et transformation du savoir administratif en France et en Allemagne (18e/19e s).* Baden-Baden, Nomos, 1989.

Hilger, Marie-Elisabeth, and Lucian Hölscher. Entries on *Kapital, Kapitalist,* and *Kapitalismus.* In *Geschichtliche Grundbegriffe,* ed. Oscar Brunner, Werner Conze, and Reinhart Koselleck, vol. 3 (1982), pp. 399–454. 8 vols. Stuttgart, Klett-Cotta, 1972–97.

Hobbes, Thomas. *Elements of Law Natural & Politic* [1640]. Ed. Ferdinand Tönnies and introduced by M. M. Goldsmith. London, Cass, 1969.

Holtfrerich, Carl-Ludwig. *Government Debt in the Economic Thought of the Long 19th Century.* Discussion Paper 2013/4, School of Business and Economics, Freie Universität, Berlin, 2013.

———. "Public Debt in Post-1850 German Economic Thought vis-à-vis the Pre-1850 British Classical School." *German Economic Review* 15 (2013): 62–83.

Hont, Istvan. "Negative Community: The Natural Law Heritage from Pufendorf to Marx." Lecture given within the John M. Olin Program in the History of Political Culture, 1 February 1989.

———. *Jealousy of Trade. International Competition and the Nation-State in Historical Perspective.* Cambridge, MA, Harvard UP, 2005.

———. *Politics in Commercial Society: Adam Smith and Jean-Jacques Rousseau.* Cambridge, MA, Harvard UP, 2015.

Hont, Istvan, and Michael Ignatieff. "Needs and Justice in the *Wealth of Nations*: An Introductory Essay." In *Wealth and Virtue: The Shaping of Political Economy in the Scottish Enlightenment,* ed. Istvan Hont and Michael Ignatieff, pp. 1–44. Cambridge, CUP, 1983.

Hunt, Lynn. *Inventing Human Rights: A History.* New York, Norton, 2007.

Husson, Jules (aka Champfleury). *Contes d'automne.* Paris, 1854.

Israel, Jonathan. *The Radical Enlightenment.* Oxford, OUP, 2001.

———. *A Revolution of the Mind: Radical Enlightenment and the Intellectual Origins of Modern Democracy.* Princeton, NJ, Princeton UP, 2010.

Jackson, Ruth Ravenscroft. *The Veiled God: Friedrich Schleiermacher's Theology of Finitude.* Leiden, Brill, 2019.

Jaume, Lucien. *Tocqueville: The Aristocratic Sources of Liberty* [2008]. Princeton, NJ, Princeton UP, 2013.

Jouanjan, Olivier. "Lorenz von Stein et les contradictions du mouvement constitutionnel révolutionnaire (1789–1794)." *Annales historiques de la révolution française* 328 (2002): 171–91.

Kalyvas, Andreas, and Ira Katznelson. "The Rhetoric of the Market: Adam Smith on Recognition, Speech and Exchange." *Review of Politics* 63 (2001): 549–79.

Kocka, Jürgen. "Capitalism: The Re-emergence of a Historical Concept." *International Social History Association Newsletter* 5 (2016): 1–26.

Kolakowski, Leszek. *Main Currents of Marxism*. 3 vols. Oxford, Clarendon Press, 1978.

Koselleck, Reinhart. *Critique and Crisis: Enlightenment and the Pathogenesis of Modern Society* [1959]. Cambridge, MA, MIT Press; Leamington Spa, UK, Berg Publishers, 1988.

Koslowski, Peter, ed. *The Theory of Ethical Economy in the Historical School*. Berlin, Springer Verlag, 1995.

Kurunmäki, Jussi, and Jani Marjanen. "Isms, Ideologies and Setting the Agenda for Public Debate." *Journal of Political Ideologies* 23 (2018): 256–82.

———. "A Rhetorical View of Isms: An Introduction." *Journal of Political Ideologies* 23 (2018): 241–55.

Kurz, Heinz D., and Neri Salvadori, eds. *The Elgar Companion to David Ricardo*. Cheltenham, UK, Edward Elgar, 2015.

Lamartine, Alphonse de. "Du droit au travail et de l'organisation du travail" [1844]. In Alphonse de Lamartine, *Œuvres, Etudes oratoires et politiques*. 2 vols. Paris, 1849.

———. *Correspondance (1807–1852)*. Ed. Valentine de Lamartine. 6 vols. Paris, 1875.

Liebich, André. *Between Ideology and Utopia*. Dordrecht, 1979.

Loubère, Leo. *Louis Blanc: His Life and His Contribution to the Rise of French Jacobin-Socialism*. Evanston, IL, Northwestern UP, 1961.

Luban, Daniel. "Adam Smith on Vanity, Domination, and History." *Modern Intellectual History* 9 (2012): 275–302.

Mackintosh, James. *A General View of the Progress of Ethical Philosophy* [1831]. Philadelphia, 1834.

Marjanen, Jani. "Ism Concepts in Science and Politics." *Contributions to the History of Concepts* 13 (2018): v–ix.

Marx, Karl, and Friedrich Engels. *The Communist Manifesto*. Ed. Gareth Stedman Jones. London, Penguin Books, 2002.

Montes, Leonidas. *Adam Smith in Context*. Basingstoke, UK, Macmillan, 2004.

Moore, Jason. *Capitalism in the Web of Life: Ecology and the Accumulation of Capital*. London, Verso, 2015.

Morice, Emile. *Révélations et pamphlets*. Paris, 1834.

Mulgan, Geoff. *The Locust and the Bee* [2013]. Princeton, NJ, Princeton UP, 2015.

Nelson, Eric. *The Greek Tradition in Republican Thought*. Cambridge, CUP, 2004.

———. *The Hebrew Republic: Jewish Sources and the Transformation of European Thought*. Cambridge, MA, Harvard UP, 2010.

Novak, Maximillian E. "Robinson Crusoe and Economic Utopia." *Kenyon Review* 25 (1963): 474–90.

Ogle, Vanessa. "Whose Time Is It? The Pluralization of Time and the Global Condition, 1870s–1940s." *American Historical Review* 118 (2013): 1376–1402.

———. "Time, Temporality and the History of Capitalism." *Past & Present* 243 (2019): 312–27.

Oncken, August. "The Consistency of Adam Smith." *Economic Journal* 7 (1897): 443–50.

———. "Das Adam Smith–Problem." *Zeitschrift fur Sozialwissenschaft* 1 (1898): 25–33, 101–8, 276–87.

Otteson, J. R. "The Recurring 'Adam Smith Problem.'" *History of Philosophy Quarterly* 17 (2000): 51–74.

Paganelli, Maria Pia. "Adam Smith and the Origins of Political Economy." *Social Philosophy and Policy* 37 (2020): 159–69.

Pasquino, Pasquale. "Introduction to Lorenz von Stein." *Economy and Society* 10 (1981): 1–6.

Passow, Richard. *Kapitalismus, eine begrifflich-terminologische Studie* [1918]. Jena, Gustav Fischer, 1927.

Paul, Helen. "David Ricardo." In *Great Economic Thinkers*, ed. Jonathan Conlin, pp. 40–53. London, Reaktion Books, 2018.

Pettit, Philip. *Republicanism: A Theory of Freedom and Government*. Oxford, OUP, 1997.

Piketty, Thomas. *Capital and Ideology*. Cambridge, MA, Belknap Press of Harvard UP, 2020.

———. Symposium: *Capital and Ideology*. Œconomia 11 (2021).

———. *Une brève histoire de l'égalité*. Paris, Seuil, 2021.

Pocock, J.G.A. *The Machiavellian Moment: Florentine Political Thought and the Atlantic Republican Tradition* [Princeton, NJ, Princeton UP, 1975]. 2nd ed. [Princeton, NJ, Princeton UP, 2003]. 3rd ed. Ed. Richard Whatmore. Princeton, NJ, Princeton UP, 2016.

Podoksik, Efraim. "Georg Simmel: Three Forms of Individualism and Historical Understanding." *New German Critique* 10 (2010): 119–45.

———. *Georg Simmel and German Culture: Unity, Variety and Modern Discontents*. Cambridge, CUP, 2021.

Pothier, Robert Joseph. *Traité du droit de domaine de propriété* [1762]. 2 vols. Paris, 1772.

Proudhon, Pierre Joseph. Notes on Pothier. Bibliothèque nationale de France, *Nouvelles acquisitions françaises*, 18258, cahier 12, "Notes sur Pothier."

———. *What Is Property?* [1840]. Ed. Donald R. Kelley and Bonnie G. Smith. Cambridge, CUP, 1994.

———. *Qu'est-ce que la propriété?* [1840]. Ed. Robert Damien and Edward Castleton. Paris, Livre de Poche, 2009.

Quante, Michael. "Positive Liberty as Realizing the Essence of Man." In *Positive Freedom, Past, Present, and Future*, ed. John Christman, pp. 28–44. Cambridge, CUP, 2022.

Reddie, James. *Inquiries Elementary and Historical in the Science of Law*. London, 1840.

Ricardo, David. *The Principles of Political Economy and Taxation*. London, 1817.

Robert, Joseph Pierre Bazile (Robert du Var). *Histoire de la classe ouvrière depuis l'esclave jusqu'au prolétaire de nos jours*. 4 vols. Paris, 1845–47.

Rosanvallon, Pierre. *Notre histoire intellectuelle et politique 1968–2018*. Paris, Seuil, 2018.

Rousseau, Jean-Jacques. *Of the Social Contract*. In Jean-Jacques Rousseau, *Collected Writings*, ed. Roger D. Masters and Christopher Kelly. 14 vols. Hanover, NH, University Press of New England, 1987–2007.

Rousseau, John James. *An Inquiry into the Nature of the Social Contract, or Principles of Political Right*. Dublin, 1791.

Runciman, David. *Pluralism and the Personality of the State*. Cambridge, CUP, 1997.

Sagar, Paul. *Adam Smith Reconsidered: History, Liberty and the Foundations of Modern Politics*. Princeton, NJ, Princeton UP, 2021.

Samuels, Warren J. "Adam Smith's 'History of Astronomy' Argument: How Broadly Does It Apply? And Where Do Propositions Which 'Sooth the Imagination' Come From?" *History of Economic Ideas* 15 (2007): 53–78.

Samuels, Warren J., and W. Henderson. "The Etiology of Adam Smith's Division of Labor: Alternative Accounts and Smith's Methodology Applied to Them." In *Essays in the History of Economics*, ed. Warren J. Samuels et al., pp. 8–89. New York, Routledge, 2004.

Savigny, Friedrich Carl von. *System des Heutigen Römischen Rechts*. Berlin, 1840.

Schleiermacher, Friedrich. *Soliloquies* [1800]. Ed. Horace Leland Friess. New York, Columbia UP, 1926.

Scott, Bruce R. *The Concept of Capitalism*. New York, Springer, 2009.

Sewell, William H., Jr. *Capitalism and the Emergence of Civic Equality in Eighteenth-Century France*. Chicago, U of Chicago Press, 2021.

Shovlin, John. *Trading with the Enemy: Britain, France and the 18th Century Quest for a Peaceful World Order*. New Haven, CT, Yale UP, 2021.

Sieyès, Emmanuel-Joseph. Manuscripts in Archives Nationales de France (= AN): AN 284 AP 2, dossier 13 (sheet headed "travail"); 284 AP 3, dossier 13; 284 AP 4, dossier 5.

———. *Political Writings*. Ed. Michael Sonenscher. Indianapolis, IN, Hackett, 2003.

Silberner, Edmond. "Le mot capitalisme." *Annales d'histoire sociale* 2 (1940): 133–34.

Simmel, Georg. *Fundamental Problems of Sociology (Individual and Society)* [1917]. In *The Sociology of Georg Simmel*, ed. Kurt H. Wolff. New York, Free Press, 1950.

Skinner, Quentin. *Liberty before Liberalism*. Cambridge, CUP, 1998.

———. *Hobbes and Republican Liberty*. Cambridge, CUP, 2008.

Smith, Adam. *Recherches sur la nature et les causes de la richesse des nations*. 4 vols. Paris, 1790.

———. *An Inquiry into the Nature and Causes of the Wealth of Nations* [1776]. 2 vols. Ed. R. H. Campbell, A. S. Skinner, and W. B. Todd. Oxford, OUP, 1976.

———. *Lectures on Jurisprudence* [1762–63]. Ed. R. L. Meek, D. D. Raphael, and P. G. Stein. Oxford, OUP, 1978.

Soliani, Riccardo, ed. *Economic Thought and Institutional Change in France and Italy (1789–1914)*. Heidelberg, Springer, 2017.

Sonenscher, Michael. *Before the Deluge: Public Debt, Inequality, and the Intellectual Origins of the French Revolution*. Princeton, NJ, Princeton UP, 2005.

———. *Jean-Jacques Rousseau: The Division of Labour, the Politics of the Imagination and the Concept of Federal Government*. Leiden, Brill, 2019.

———. *The Romans, the Germans and the Moderns: An Essay on the Foundations of Modern Politics*. Princeton, NJ, Princeton UP, forthcoming.

Stedman Jones, Gareth. *Karl Marx: Greatness and Illusion*. London, Allen Lane, 2016.

Stein, Lorenz von. *Geschichte der sozialen Bewegung in Frankreich von 1789 bis auf unsere Tage*. Leipzig, 1850.

———. *Lehrbuch der Finanzwissenschaft*. Leipzig, 1871.

———. *Le concept de société*. Trans. Marc Béghin. Ed. Norbert Waszek. Grenoble, ELLUG, 2002.

Stepelevich, Lawrence S., ed. *The Young Hegelians: An Anthology*. Cambridge, CUP, 1983.

Stewart, Dugald. *An Account of the Life and Writings of Adam Smith* [1793]. In *Biographical Memoirs of Adam Smith, William Robertson and Thomas Reid*, ed. Sir William Hamilton. Edinburgh, 1858.

Tortajada, Ramón, ed. *The Economics of Sir James Steuart*. London, Routledge, 1999.

Tribe, Keith. "'Das Adam Smith Problem' and the Origins of Modern Smith Scholarship." *History of European Ideas* 34 (2008): 514–25.

———. *The Economy of the Word: Language, History, and Economics*. Oxford, OUP, 2015.

———. "The 'System of Natural Liberty': Natural Order in the *Wealth of Nations*." *History of European Ideas* 47 (2021): 573–83.

Tuck, Richard. *Philosophy and Government 1572–1651*. Cambridge, CUP, 1993.

———. *The Sleeping Sovereign: The Invention of Modern Democracy*. Cambridge, CUP, 2015.

Ulas Ince, Onur. *Colonial Capitalism and the Dilemmas of Liberalism*. Oxford, OUP, 2018.

United States Reports. *Cases Adjudged in the Supreme Court at October Term, 1895*. New York, 1896.

Van der Linden, Marcel, and Karl Heinz Roth, eds. *Beyond Marx: Theorizing the Global Labour Relations of the Twenty-First Century*. Leiden, Brill, 2014.

Villeneuve, Pons Louis Frédéric, marquis de. *De l'agonie de la France* [1835]. 2nd ed. 2 vols. Paris, 1839.

Walicki, Andrej. *Philosophy and Romantic Nationalism: The Case of Poland*. Oxford, OUP, 1982.

———. *Russia, Poland, and Universal Regeneration*. Notre Dame, IN, U of Notre Dame Press, 1991.

Wallerstein, Immanuel. *The Modern World System*. 3 vols. New York, Academic Press, 1974–89.

———, ed. *The Modern World-System in the* Longue Durée [2004]. Oxford, Routledge, 2016.

Walter, Ryan. *Before Method and Models: The Political Economy of Malthus and Ricardo*. Oxford, OUP, 2021.

Waszek, Norbert. "L'état de droit social chez Lorenz von Stein." In *Figures de l'état de droit: Le Rechtsstaat dans l'histoire intellectuelle et constitutionnelle de l'Allemagne*, ed. Olivier Jouanjan, pp. 193–217. Strasbourg, Presses universitaires de Strasbourg, 2001.

INDEX

acquisitive society, 161

administration, 18, 95, 118, 119–23, 125–26, 140, 151, 155, 163–64; and constitution, 156, 157; and public debt, 126, 151. *See also* Hegel; Stein

Allonville, Armand François, comte d', 40, 42, 48

altruism, 96

anarchy, 84. *See also* Proudhon

assignat, 151

Austrian Succession, War of, 31

autonomy, 79, 110, 114, 158. *See also* division of labour

Avril, Victor, 57

Balzac, Honoré de, 32

Bastiat, Frédéric, 56–57, 61–63, 70

Beauchamp, Alphonse de, 40

Belgium, independence of, 32–38; debt, 35–36; trade of, 34–37

Bentham, Jeremy, 22, 107

Berlin, Isaiah, 22

Blackstone, William, 79

Blanc, Louis, x–xii, xv, xvi, 51, 53, 54–58, 61, 63, 66–67, 69, 72, 98, 146, 166–67

Blanqui, Adolphe, 56

Bloch, Marc, x

Bodin, Jean, 22

Bonald, Louis de, xiv–xv, xvi, 45–48

Bonaparte, Louis Napoleon, 57

Bonapartism, 51

Brentano, Lujo, 97

Britain, 34, 36, 45, 71, 127, 144; Bonald on, 45–48; Montesquieu on, 47–48; party politics in, 127–28

A NOTE ON THE TYPE

This book has been composed in Arno, an Old-style serif
typeface in the classic Venetian tradition, designed by
Robert Slimbach at Adobe.